DIGITAL LEARNING FOR ALL *now*

A School Leader's Guide for 1:1 on a Budget

JONATHAN P. COSTA, SR.

Foreword by Kenneth R. Freeston

CORWIN
A SAGE Company

CORWIN
A SAGE Company

FOR INFORMATION:

Corwin
A SAGE Company
2455 Teller Road
Thousand Oaks, California 91320
(800) 233-9936
Fax: (800) 417-2466
www.corwin.com

SAGE Ltd.
1 Oliver's Yard
55 City Road
London EC1Y 1SP
United Kingdom

SAGE India Pvt. Ltd.
B 1/I 1 Mohan Cooperative
Industrial Area
Mathura Road, New Delhi 110 044
India

SAGE Asia-Pacific Pte. Ltd.
33 Pekin Street #02-01
Far East Square
Singapore 048763

Acquisitions Editor: Debra Stollenwerk
Associate Editor: Desirée A. Bartlett
Editorial Assistant: Kimberly Greenberg
Project Editor: Veronica Stapleton
Copy Editor: Matthew Sullivan
Typesetter: C&M Digitals (P) Ltd.
Proofreader: Jennifer Gritt
Indexer: Jean Casalegno
Cover Designer: Karine Hovsepian
Permissions Editor: Adele Hutchinson

Copyright © 2012 by Corwin

Printed in the United States of America.

Library of Congress Cataloging-in-Publication Data

Costa, Jonathan P.

Digital learning for all, now : a school leader's guide for 1:1 on a budget / Jonathan P. Costa, Sr.; foreword by Kenneth R. Freeston.

p. cm.
Includes bibliographical references and index.

ISBN 978-1-4522-2005-5 (pbk.)

1. Internet in education. 2. Education—Effect of technological innovations on. 3. Digital communications. 4. Education—Aims and objectives. 5. Educational leadership. I. Title.

LB1044.87.C677 2012
371.33′44678—dc23   2011048361

This book is printed on acid-free paper.

Certified Chain of Custody
Promoting Sustainable Forestry
www.sfiprogram.org
SFI-01268

SFI label applies to text stock

12 13 14 15 16 10 9 8 7 6 5 4 3 2 1

DIGITAL LEARNING FOR ALL *now*

*To Mom for her unconditional support and for my love of books.
To Dad for teaching me the meaning of the family business and
for a lifetime with all things Royal and Ancient.
To Wendy for 25 years of love, encouragement, and
tolerance of all my pursued obsessions. And finally, to
Jonathan and Carl who both make us proud every day.*

Contents

Additional materials and resources related to *Digital Learning For All, Now: A School Leaders' Guide for 1:1 on a Budget* can be found at **http//www.digitallearningforallnow.com**

List of Tables and Illustrations

Chapter 1

Chapter 2

Chapter 3

Chapter 4

Chapter 5

Chapter 6

Foreword

Institutions and societies prosper when innovation is encouraged and honored. As a culture and a people, we were innovating centuries before we knew anything about digital learning. Today, with technology seamlessly integrating into our lives, we have dramatic new opportunities for increased innovation that can sustain us through the 21st century and beyond.

To realize this potential, we have an imperative as a society to understand technology and make it thoughtfully available everywhere, to everyone. It is the new electricity. As an essential utility of learning, its presence in every part of our students' lives today compels us to think differently about the relationship between the educational system, digital learning, and innovation.

Students enter schools across the country with technology already integrated into their own ways of interacting with their world and are primed to be taught to use it for productive purposes. They are digital natives ready to solve problems through critical and creative thinking. They thrive in digital learning environments and, with guidance, can use the new tools of innovation designed for their generation.

Yet, we live in a time of a voracious governmental appetite for pencil and paper standardized test scores that rank and sort students, and judge schools and even teachers based on metrics that we know are less and less aligned with the future skills that students will need to be successful. These mandates from the print-based past have a chilling effect on our innovative spirit. And, as many of us know too, well, even in schools and communities where there is a general will to break this pattern and expand access to student and teacher use of technology, often the details, costs, and logistics of putting a plan into action snarl the initiative. At this critical time when educational leaders desperately need a new way to think about how to bridge the gap between what is and what needs to be, what is desired is a thoughtful resource that illuminates a way forward.

Jonathan Costa is a visionary leader, practitioner, thinker, and innovator, and he has provided such a pathway in his new book, *Digital Learning for All, Now*. Since before our first professional collaboration began more than 20 years ago, Jonathan has consistently demonstrated an understanding of technology's role as a change agent that betrays his digital immigrant status. He has worked with my staff and those of numerous other districts across the country to expand their thinking about the potential for these new tools for learning. As you will see in this terrific book, he not only engages the reader through this range of experiences to build a compelling rationale for why digital is the future of teaching and learning, but he also shares practical strategies to help school leaders begin the process of transformation within their own learning organizations. This systems shift is the first step to unleashing a wave of innovation in your schools, classrooms, and student learners.

Any superintendent, district or building leader, policy maker, or education advocate will benefit from Jonathan's expertise as displayed in the ideas presented in *Digital Learning for All, Now*. His direct and focused narrative takes the complex work of understanding digital learning and encouraging innovation for leaders, teachers, and students and makes it understandable, manageable, and affordable. This book and its companion digital resources are a marriage of theory and practice that can serve as a "Google Map" for all those seeking to grow the integration of digital learning into their schools. The messages in *Digital Learning for All, Now* are timely. Urgent. Buy this book; start your own innovations now.

Dr. Kenneth R. Freeston

With nearly forty years of experience as an educator, author, and photographer, Ken Freeston is currently the superintendent of schools in North Salem, New York. Prior to coming to North Salem, he served as the superintendent of schools in Ridgefield and Redding, Connecticut. He has twice been named Educational Leader of the Year by statewide and regional associations and is an active member in Ken Kay's EdLeader21's efforts to advocate for innovation in education.

Preface

Potential Within Reach

It is just common sense. All around, the evidence is undeniable and abundant: We live in a world that depends on digital content and resources as the primary tools for learning and work. A new era is upon us, and the concurrent demands of 21st century learning grow by the year. In such an environment, one would think that public schools, the institution with the greatest burden of preparing students for this reality, would aggressively shift resources to get every learner a digital device. This vision is known as *1:1 learning*. Instead of forty-pound backpacks stuffed with books, students would carry a laptop, netbook, tablet, or some other mobile device that allows them to access the information they need to construct knowledge from anywhere at any time. How better to acclimate the student to the conditions that will be required for their success?

Unfortunately, this inevitable transition has been so slow in its development. At least a decade after it was practically possible, just a small fraction of public schools have the 1:1 technology access that is required to make it happen. Even in communities where there is a will to change, a few stubborn barriers have consistently blocked progress. Among the most prominent are an economic climate that seems to preclude even the consideration of buying every student a capable electronic device and a dearth of practical strategies for how to guide a school system through the transition from print to digital learning.

The negative power of these obstacles and a growing sense of urgency for breakthrough solutions are the driving forces behind the creation of *Digital Learning for All, Now*. I have spent the last twenty-five years working with educators and innovators who are dedicated to crafting a learning environment that appropriately prepares students for their future. The lessons learned from these experiences and recent technology advances have finally opened the lock. The time to act is now; the future is truly within our grasp.

Why *Digital Learning for All, Now* Is Different From Other Books on the Market

Digital Learning for All, Now provides superintendents, assistant superintendents, district-level instructional supervisors, technology directors, teacher leaders, as well as other interested stakeholders and policy makers with more than just platitudes and exhortations. This resource has integrated the "why" with the strategies and solutions needed to overcome the affordability and systems-change problems that have heretofore prevented the public school instructional transformation to 1:1 learning. It is designed to be a comprehensive and flexible read that recognizes the importance of 21st century learning, demonstrates how to acquire and pay for the required equipment, and then maps out how to change the instructional system and culture to maximize the benefit to students.

The result is that *Digital Learning for All, Now* takes *purpose-driven* systems thinking and directly connects it to *practical and cost-effective* processes to make it work. To accomplish this, *Digital Learning for All, Now* guides readers through three content domains that will give them equal doses of vision, motivation, and practical support for purposeful guided action. In addition, it gives readers access to online resources and a community of educators who share the same goals.

Part I: Why We Need *Digital Learning for All, Now*

To help educators build momentum and make the case for change, Part I of *Digital Learning for All, Now* revisits and reinforces the need for the transformation of public school instruction. It begins by emphatically stating that the center of gravity in the debate has shifted from a discussion over whether or not a move to 1:1 makes sense to deciding what is the best way to get there and what you should do once your school arrives. To demonstrate this, the narrative will explore how those of us who are responsible for the leadership of public schools are increasingly frustrated by the obvious lack of alignment between what needs to be and what currently is. We are more than a decade into the 21st century, the world around us is being constantly redefined by emerging digital processes, and yet, the vast majority of public schools grind away in a learning model defined by print. How can public schools meet the challenges of the modern learner when they are consistently using tools unchanged since Gutenberg?

The truth is they can't. We understand that without 1:1 technology access, the full potential of information age instructional opportunity is stunted. We know equally well that with current school financing constraints, few districts can afford to buy every student an appropriate device, which is the first critical step of this journey. Finally, and most distressingly, we know that without a 1:1 device's empowering impact on learners, engaging instructional practices that support appropriate preparation for 21st century learning will remain the exception, not the rule.

Achieving 1:1 status is critical because it is the pathway to access. In a 21st century 1:1 classroom, all students have an Internet-capable device that they use to own their learning. This access and sense of ownership is what enables the shift in focus of the classroom process from the teacher to the learner. So important and mainstream is this topic, it has been recognized as critical by national policy makers as well. The U.S. Department of Education's National Technology Plan (2010) states that the nation's educational priorities should be "to engage and empower students, measure what matters, prepare and connect everyone, and enable these changes through redesign and transformation of the public school system."

Part II: Getting to 1:1

With the need for 1:1 illustrated, Part II of *Digital Learning for All, Now* describes in three chapters what I call the *open path*: a series of open-source and crowd-sourcing supply options that will allow every school district to affordably accomplish the move to 1:1 learning. In addition to a reasoned and logical theoretical structure, this entire section is loaded with information, tools, and strategies that make 1:1 possible. And most importantly, they show how, in most cases, 1:1 can be achieved given only a school or district's existing budget. In just Chapters 2–4, you will find

- exclusive access information for the *Digital Learning for All, Now* online user community;
- strategies for advocating for bring your own device (BYOD) throughout your learning community;
- comprehensive examinations of the key barriers that block progress and strategies for making the change to 1:1 happen;
- complete BYOD preplanning templates to make the transition happen;
- links to open-source operating systems, back-office applications, and productivity software that are free and functional;
- software migration and change strategies to help integrate these resources effectively;
- print spending analysis tools for determining actual per pupil print instructional costs and identifying how much money can be saved;
- links to free digital textbook alternatives to reduce dependence on print textbooks;
- links to hundreds of instructional resource pages in every content area;
- links to entire user communities dedicated to open-source resources in education;
- strategies that support an organizational transition to open-source instructional materials;
- strategies for improving instructional and technology integration;
- strategies for supporting differentiated and customized instruction through technology;
- sample acceptable use policies and strategies for supporting 1:1 implementations across a district; and
- strategies for managing risk and ensuring long-term 1:1 success.

Part III: Building the System

The last section of the book recognizes that putting a device in the hands of every student is a good start, but it is only the first step of many. Experience demonstrates that building a truly engaging and rigorous 21st century learning environment takes more than just molded plastic and silicone chips. Additional and important shifts are needed in instructional design, delivery, and assessment to transform teaching and learning from a print to a digital learning orientation. Chapters 5 and 6 serve as a guidebook for making those difficult but critical changes. The resources and strategies in this section include

- foundational assumptions of 1:1 digital learning environments;
- explanations of the support systems for 21st century learning;
- priority 21st century skills and assessment guidance;
- samples of district mission statement and support documents;
- authentic 21st century task instructional design templates;
- sample 21st century skill assessment rubrics;
- leadership for 21st century skills self-reflection grids;
- sample change process maps;
- an information literacy reliable resources research grid; and
- a comprehensive three-phase implementation framework for BYOD and 1:1.

The impact of this third section of the book extends beyond digital learning and 21st century skills. By following the systems alignment and improvement strategies in *Digital Learning for All, Now*, districts will find their ability to systemically improve instruction and rigor on any goal for learning increase. This will assist in any district's concurrent efforts to prepare for the implementation of Common Core State Standards and its associated new generation of assessments.

Digital Learning for All, Now: More Than Just a Book

There is an accepted irony that in some ways, *Digital Learning for All, Now* is a textbook about the end of textbooks. That would be hard to defend if the available resources started and ended with the just the book; they don't. *Digital Learning for All, Now* has a robust and significant online presence that will provide educational leaders with access to numerous electronic resources that support the implementation of the strategies outlined in the book. All of the aforementioned tools have downloadable versions available to readers through the *Digital Learning for All, Now* user site. So not only can you learn about how to use the tools through the book, but you will also be able to go the web, download them, and actually use them in your own district-change process. Additionally, through the user community blogs and postings, you will be able to learn real-time lessons from others who are on the same journey.

Additionally, throughout the entire text, there are regularly placed reflection and study questions. These provocative questions are designed to give readers discussion points from which to engage their peers and constituents on the key issues that underlie the book.

Through these interactions, school leaders and change agents will gain insight regarding their own thinking and the mindsets of others. This information can then be used to build understanding and improve the chances of successful change. From the first printed page through all of the numerous electronic resources, *Digital Learning for All, Now* helps you put your own theory into practice.

Every Journey Begins With One Step

Digital Learning for All, Now is a narrative that combines the motivation to realign public schooling with the practical strategies that are required for bridging the equipment, policy, and cultural gaps that have usually blocked systems change. When applied with constancy of purpose and adapted to a local context, the processes defined in *Digital Learning for All, Now* will facilitate the transition from print to 21st century digital learning on a districtwide scale, effectively creating an instructional setting that prepares every student for life, learning, and work in the 21st century.

So, if you are ready for schools that more effectively prepare students for the future while saving money over time, then you are ready to take the journey. Let's get started!

Acknowledgments

I want to first acknowledge Nancy Love for twenty years of professional collaborations, for her spirit, and for helping me take that first step. To my executive director at EDUCATION CONNECTION, Dr. Dani Thibodeau—thank you for your support of my career, your unwavering encouragement of *Digital Learning for All, Now*, and for teaching me the meaning of "nuts and bolts." I will always be grateful for Dr. Russ Coward's generous mentoring of my writing and to Laurie Sweet for all of her wonderful assistance with the graphic elements of this project. Finally, to my Corwin Editor, Debra Stollenwerk— thank you for your enthusiastic advocacy of *Digital Learning for All, Now*, for your thoughtful editorial guidance, and for the patience required to guide a new author through this process.

Publisher's Acknowledgments

Corwin gratefully acknowledges the following individuals for taking the time to provide their editorial feedback and guidance:

Amie Brown, Teacher
Armuchee Middle School
Armuchee, GA

Barbara Cavanah, District
    Webmaster, District Grade-
    book Manager, Teacher
Marathon High School
Marathon, FL

J-Petrina McCarty-Puhl,
    Teacher
Robert McQueen High School
Reno, NV

Rick Miller, Superintendent
Riverside Unified School
    District
Riverside, CA

Tanna Nicely, Assistant Principal
Dogwood Elementary
Knoxville, TN

Lyndon Oswald, Principal
Sandcreek Middle School
Ammon, ID

Renee Peoples, Teacher
West Elementary School
Bryson City, NC

About the Author

Litchfield Hills
Photography

Jonathan P. Costa, Sr. is the Director of School and Program Services for EDUCATION CONNECTION, a regional education service center in Litchfield, Connecticut. A former public and private school social studies teacher, educational consultant, and businessman, Mr. Costa's current responsibilities include supervision of the highly regarded Center for 21st Century Skills and the delivery of all professional development and consulting interventions on behalf of his agency throughout the tri-state area. Through his years of educational service, he has provided close support for strategic and technology planning in dozens of districts, guided all manner of instructional improvements, and consulted on the promotion, identification, definition, instruction, and assessment of 21st century skills. Mr. Costa is a frequent speaker at regional and national conferences, and his writings have appeared in publications as varied as *Educational Leadership* and *Runner's World*.

Married to Wendy, his wife of twenty-five years, together they have two sons and a Labrador retriever that ensure constant movement and an endless array of active and interesting life experiences. Beyond his family and work responsibilities, Jonathan maintains a scratch handicap on the golf course and spends the rest of his free time pursuing his passions for running, strength training, yoga, and cycling.

PART I

Why We Need *Digital Learning for All, Now*

1

Beyond a Doubt

Digital Is the Future of Teaching and Learning

Starting With the End in Mind

As with any successful process that aims to create or support significant change, a journey to transform schools must be purpose driven.
What is the mission of public schooling? Without clarity of the eventual goal, whatever action is undertaken will be untethered to purpose and thus unlikely to succeed.

The driving force for public schools has always been grounded on
an egalitarian value. As Western civilization emerged from a "might
makes right" dynamic to a shared ethic that "all people have rights,"
there naturally emerged a need for a common system to ensure that
everyone had the tools to understand these rights and exercise them
properly (Cubberly, 1919). As such, since our founding, preparation
of all students and the continuation of our democracy have served as
the dual foundations of public schools in the United States.

With these assumptions as background, we might reasonably ask,
preparation for what? The answer for the last several generations has
been preparation of students for their lives, learning, and work
beyond the classroom. As public schools have evolved over time, the

consensus mission that has emerged is that in to be worth their investment, education institutions need to ensure that all students acquire the knowledge and skills that are required for them to be successful and productive citizens. Having facilitated dozens of mission-creation discussions in public high schools over the last twenty-five years, I have used the "What are the knowledge and skills?" question to frame each community's answer.

As a reflection of the society they serve, it is instructive to watch how the answers to the proper-preparation question have changed. The first public schools were established primarily to ensure that every student could read the Bible. With the advent of the Industrial Revolution, we saw the emergence of the famous "3 Rs": Reading, wRiting, and aRithmetic. So influential and constant were these three foundations that they remain the most tested and reported on academic reference points to this day.

But what is the answer for the 21st century? Currently, what passes for basic skills must be redefined in the context of what is needed for successful participation in an information-saturated and hyper-adaptive digital world. Certainly, some skills are timeless in their necessity, but anyone who believes that the skills required for life in the 19th or 20th centuries will be adequate in 2025 or beyond needs to think carefully about what has recently unfolded in the world around us.

Truth 1: The Future of Learning and Work Is Digital

The Pace of Technology Change

It is easy to forget how much of the structure of learning and knowledge access has been altered during our lifetimes. Such is the pace of change in a technology society ruled by Moore's Law where every eighteen months, device capacity doubles and prices drop (Intel, 2010). Peers on my first public school faculty delighted in telling me about how in the spring of 1969, teachers lined up outside the main office of Housatonic Valley Regional High School to wait their turn to use a miracle device that would save them time in the figuring of their students' final grade averages: a $500 Sharp QT-8 four-function calculator. We find digital devices with 10,000 times more computational capability as giveaway prizes in cereal boxes today.

We have become so accustomed to the rapid assimilation of successive waves of technology advancement that we take for granted how dramatic the accumulated scope of the change actually is. To graph the progression of microchip processor power over the last forty years, a straight line on an upward sixty-five-degree angle would be a good representation. Known as *Moore's Law* after Gordon Moore of Intel predicted this ascension, so dramatic has this experience been that Intel itself has started to use metaphors to help people appreciate how far things have come in so short a time. Figure 1.1 is titled "If transistors were people" and speaks to how many more processing units they are able to fit on the standard central processing unit chip today as compared to when they started manufacturing them in the early 1970s.

Figure 1.1   Visualizing Progress—Moore's Law

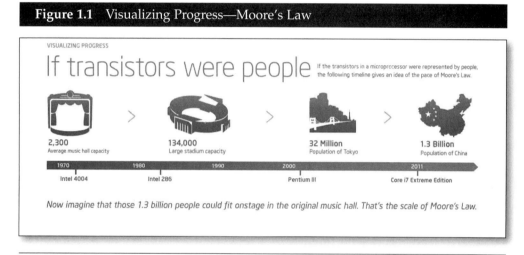

Source: Intel, 2010. Reprinted with permission. Retrieved from http://www.intel.com/technology/mooreslaw/

We see the greatest impact of these changes in our youth. The current generation of teenage high school students not only missed the heyday of the phonograph, but some are also probably blissfully unaware of all three successive generations of devices that replaced it: the eight-track, the cassette tape, and the CD. They have never known a phone that needed to be plugged into anything but a charger. They have no memory of a time when a person could not be instantly connected to anyone they cared about the second that they had the idea to do so. Forget hand-written anything, this is the same generation that forsakes e-mail because it is too slow. As one of my colleagues observed regarding his texting teens, "If you had told me in 1980 that I would raise two school-age daughters and never hear a phone ring, I would have told you, you were nuts."

New devices go from being "must haves" to quaint relics in a matter of months. Such is life in the digital world. It would be easy to dismiss these examples as a whimsical consumer electronics phenomenon only and miss the larger point. The capabilities inherent in these devices are forever changing the way we learn and work and have implications for any institution that seeks to prepare students for life within this world. To see this illustrated, just turn to any institution that was born in the analogue era and see how it has adapted, or not, to these new digital circumstances. Newspapers, the post office, Blockbuster, the reference section of your local library—all of these are easy-to-find examples of products and services made obsolete by the advance of technology. On the other side of the ledger are those entities that were made possible by these same changes.

The Rise of the Information Age

To this end, consider the emergence and growing influence of Google. In Google, we can see the arc of a company's development untouched by print, as they were conceived, grew, and now thrive in a purely digital context. In Google's short fifteen-year history, the impact of their work has done more to challenge assumptions related to knowledge and learning than anything since the printing press. Just as Gutenberg brought the printed word to a much broader audience, Google has facilitated and accelerated the digitization of the world's factual knowledge and pioneered processes to make this information accessible to everyone.

Elegant in its simplicity, Google's mission is "to organize the world's information and make it universally accessible and useful" (Google, 2009). So successful has Google been in this pursuit that their search processes have famously crossed over into the popular culture as a verb. Want to find something? You don't *web search* for it, you *Google it*. Google co-founder Larry Page has described the "perfect search engine" as something that "understands exactly what you mean and gives you back exactly what you want" (Google, 2009). While it might feel just a little Orwellian, everyone that has ever used the Google search engine knows exactly what this means. You have a query, you start typing/speaking, a list of possible matches appears, and with each character or word you type/say, the list narrows until your answer or a useful link appears. Brilliant.

Perhaps more than any other digitally inspired company, Google's zeal to achieve their mission has helped build, open, and then widen the information floodgates. As providers of similar search engine services (Microsoft, Yahoo, etc.) try to innovate and keep up with Google's frenetic development pace, their combined efforts have ensured that the center of gravity for factual knowledge has shifted from print sources to digital access before our eyes.

Access Is the First Step

Once the move to digitize was underway, it developed its own momentum. Knowledge truly is power. When I know something you don't know and that thing has value, eventually I am going to be the winner, and you are going to be the loser. As capital markets began to understand that digital information meant having valuable things before anyone else and how that early access could be converted into profits, the fate of the printed page was sealed. Like a car rolling downhill without brakes, once the move to gain financial advantage by speeding up the knowledge process got going, there was nothing that could be done to stop it. Anyone who resists or steps into the runaway vehicle's path is given credit for bravery but is quickly crushed by its force.

Predictably, even when this trend toward searchable and ready facts was apparent, many traditionalists refused to acknowledge the change or constructed alternative realities to fit their mindset. Certainly, a knowledgeable person in a good library could find things as efficiently as someone who was tied to a workstation in the computer lab. Perhaps there would at least be a balance and a role for traditional books that could sustain print for another generation, yes? Alas, if there was any hope for this last stand to succeed the advent of truly mobile, handheld access to all of this ready data was the digital knowledge Rubicon.

In 2005, the early days of search mobility, I remember being among the first in my social and work circles to use my Palm Treo and Google mobile to retrieve stuff from the Internet to settle arguments or satisfy curiosities. At that time, because I was an early adopter, it was a novel exercise that was thrilling to me and I am sure annoying to others. But as mobile web access went mainstream and the crowd got onboard, this process grew from a sideshow to the main act. I now expect that with my iPhone, I can find whatever I need, whether it be information to assist in work, life, or family activities, to conduct my affairs from wherever I am at the moment I want to do it.

This expectation for vocational and personal hyper-connectivity is the new driving energy of the information age. According to Alexa (2011), the top ten web traffic sites worldwide in the first half of 2011 are all either information search or social network sharing sites. Worldwide Internet pathways facilitate billions of information exchanges every hour.

This demonstrates that the world has become one massive information-sharing network, with enormous numbers of people relentlessly seeking, gathering, and sharing information in real time. This is how Twitter went from its launch and the first "tweet" in July 2006 to delivering tweet number 350 billion just five years later ("Twitter Delivers," 2011). Change on this level cannot occur without social consequences. As access has exploded, so have constructions around the expertise, status, and credentialing that used to be associated with accumulated factual knowledge. Traditional academic stratifications have always been built and secured in part by access to knowledge: the limitations on what books people could read or were allowed to use. Tuition purchased access to professorial expertise and accumulated library knowledge. The "expert" was identified as such because she spent years gathering and storing information that few others had access to.

Figure 1.2 Top Ten Internet Traffic Sites as of June 30, 2011

1. Google	6. Baidu
2. Facebook	7. Wikipedia
3. YouTube	8. Windows Live
4. Yahoo	9. Twitter
5. Blogger	10. QQ.com

Source: Alexa, 2011.

Raising the Performance Bar

No more. With digitization has come the great democratization of factual knowledge. The common ruck has just as much access to the world's digital information as the most learned expert. With a device that costs less than a pair of fancy sneakers, any learner can access almost any piece of data whenever he wants it. As a result, as facts have become ubiquitous, like any other supply and demand commodity, their value as a currency in the knowledge market has declined.

If anyone can find any fact from anywhere at any time, doing so becomes the norm, and the attention shifts from what you know to what can be done with what you know. So what if you know it or can find it; anyone can do that. Can you add value to it, can you communicate it, can you share it, can you inspire with it? Authors like Tom Friedman (2011) and Daniel Pink (2005) have written brilliantly on this topic, and it is this dynamic that should be raising the "basic skills" bar for educators and schools and driving increased learner expectations.

Unfortunately, there are those who fall back on convention and propose that the answer to factual saturation is to double down and add even more of the same onto already impossibly overloaded curricula. How else to explain curriculum maps that assume the acquisition of multiple knowledge standards every day and require "pacing guides" to ensure that proper coverage takes place? In an era when you had to carry everything you needed in your head, this kind of "just in case" mentality—as in, "We will teach this to you just in case you may need it at some as yet to be determined point in the future"—was an important curriculum touchstone. As the world's foundational knowledge has grown geometrically, so has the pressure to expand the size and contents of the just-in-case curricula. What follows, then, are increasingly absurd attempts to transfer it all into student brains in the same 180-day, knowledge-cramming window we have always called the school year.

Ultimately, this is a futile pursuit because being able to just know or find lots of stuff is not enough. Today, to be considered a valuable knowledge worker, you must be able to find what you need on a just-in-time basis. You need to sort out the meaningful from the meaningless, make new connections between seemingly random data sets, and then creatively align learning process with intended purposes. What used to be considered the foundation of knowledge work, the accumulation of facts and details, is now outsourced through technological processes. In his groundbreaking book *A Whole New Mind*, Daniel Pink (2005) describes this shifting phenomenon as "the three A's": Asia, abundance, and automation. Pink makes the case that with the huge numbers of factually knowledgeable people, the abundance of quality options, and the automation of low-level knowledge processes, significant value-added work must be at the conceptual and creative level.

REFLECTION/STUDY QUESTION

Have you felt the tension between "just in case" and "just in time" in curriculum deliberations? What is the current state of the debate in your community? Has the introduction of knowledge-gathering devices and ubiquitous information access shifted the discussion about how much constitutes enough in a deliberation over what students actually need to know to be productive?

Knowing Is No Longer Enough: 21st Century Skills

With technology and access to the world's knowledge, getting the factual level answer correct is now assumed. It is what happens next that will determine your ability to add value. This approach should not be confused with an argument that content and rigor does not matter. Of course they do: Skill without any knowledge foundation is useless, and skill application without rigorous standards of quality is just busywork. We need to know enough to give us context.

This is more of a productivity issue, how and how well you gather the facts you need before you take action. In any enterprise, ignoring technology-enabled leaps in productivity in favor of tradition may have a romantic allure and satisfy a nostalgic urge, but you cannot follow that path and expect to remain competitive in the marketplace. A farmer who plows, plants, and picks by hand may have our respect, but he is unlikely to have our business simply based on the volume of goods he is able to produce when compared to his peers riding tractors and using conveyors. Similarly, in an ever-rising information tide, you either learn how to swim or you drown.

Keeping today's students afloat in a just-in-time digital world is the reason for the growing interest and focus on what have become commonly labeled *21st century skills*. A quick literature search with that term will immediately demonstrate the weight of this attention. Over the last decade, there have been hundreds of articles and studies directed at either identifying 21st century skills or advocating for their elevation to core curriculum status. As an example of the sense of urgency now aligned with this topic, starting in 2011, the secondary school accreditation organization in New England (New England Association for Schools and Colleges, 2011) requires all applying high schools to identify academic, civic, and social learning expectations under the banner of 21st century skills.

So, what exactly are 21st century skills? In the broadest sense, they can be summarized as the information literacy, communications, problem-solving, and creative attributes needed for success in a dynamically changing learning environment. They differ from a list we might have created a hundred or fifty years ago due to the starting assumptions about knowledge access and the modern importance of being able to effectively sort through multitudes of potential sources and points of view.

To gain the specificity needed to actually teach and assess these skills, we need to dig a little deeper. Since 2004, my own organization, EDUCATION CONNECTION, has hosted our own Center for 21st Century Skills. This first of its kind training center was created to provide public school students with models of exemplary, self-directed learning experiences built on solid content foundations. In our center, we work with teachers from our member districts to create challenge-based, Moodle-hosted, blended learning curricula that engage students in the development and practice of 21st century skills. As a result, we have been recognized with funding by the U.S. Department of Education's Investing in Innovation program and by the National Science Foundation for our ability to identify, teach, and assess these skills.

When we started the conversation with educators about how to identify specific 21st century skills to use as a focus of our programming, we began by reviewing much of the contextual material that started this chapter. With that as a starting point, we then looked to others who have done similar exercises to compare findings. Much has been written over the last decade or so on this topic, so there was plenty of data to work with. For our reference, we compared our thinking with what we believed to be the three most important recent compilation studies of 21st century skills: the North Central Regional Education Laboratory's *enGauge: 21st Century Skills* (NCREL, 2003), the International Society for Technology Education's National Technology Standards (ISTE, 2008), and Ken Kay's 21st Century Skills Partnership (http://www.p21.org/, 2004). With all of this information to work with, we completed a crosswalk of these three studies.

The result of this exercise was a list of what we believe to be the six most important 21st century skills. We limited it to six out of dozens of possible skills because we believe, as will become apparent as we move through these chapters, that focus is important. A district that is attempting to teach and assess for twenty or forty different skills will soon discover that by spreading their energies, they end up doing few of them as well as is needed. We have found that starting with a core of six helps our participating districts begin the process of understanding and explicitly integrating 21st century skill competencies into everyday instruction. A complete description of these skills with assessment guidance is available for download at the *Digital Learning for All, Now* website. Directions for accessing and downloading this and all of the other resources on that site are listed in the next chapter.

Whether you start with one of the studies we used, find another, start from scratch, or use the skills crosswalk we developed, I am confident you will find that there is an implicit recognition that it is the process of integrating, connecting, and creating new knowledge/ value and then communicating the outcome that is the consensus framework of knowledge work in the 21st century. If your district has been working on integrating Common Core State Standards, you will find a similar set of assumptions underlying the content delivery of these as well. A more complete description of what an educational system based on this framework looks like is explored in Chapters 5 and 6 of this book.

Figure 1.3   Six Critical 21st Century Skills

EDUCATION CONNECTION'S
Center for 21st Century Skills Crosswalk

- Use real-world digital and other research tools to access, evaluate, and effectively apply information appropriate for authentic tasks.
- Work independently and collaboratively to solve problems and accomplish goals.
- Communicate information clearly and effectively using a variety of tools/media in varied contexts for a variety of purposes.
- Demonstrate innovation, flexibility, and adaptability in thinking patterns, work habits, and working/learning conditions.
- Effectively apply the analysis, synthesis, and evaluative processes that enable productive problem solving.
- Value and demonstrate personal responsibility, character, cultural understanding, and ethical behavior.

If the historical narrative about the transition from print to digital is not enough to convince you about the veracity of Truth 1, then the accumulating scholarship, effort, and consensus regarding the need for focus on 21st century skills should do it. Across the broadest spectrum of professional educational work over the past decade, the consensus is overwhelming: The future of learning and work is digital. I would offer one possible twist. It is not the future of learning and work that is going to be digital as much as the focus of learning and work is *already* digital. Truth 1 in *Digital Learning for All, Now* is not a prediction of the future; it is an observation of present fact.

As such, if preparation for life beyond school is the focus of a public school's mission, then all schools need to make it their primary goal to ensure that every learner has access to the instructional experiences, information, and resources needed to prepare them for learning, life, and work in the 21st century. I believe that achieving this goal is the defining educational challenge of our time, and everyone must recognize that it can only be accomplished by acquiring the proper tools that enable its occurrence. There is no need to just take only my word to support this position, nor should you think that this is simply a fancy of left-leaning educator's search for the next big thing. From conservative thinkers like Jeb Bush and his Digital Learning Council to the U.S. Department of Education's National Technology Plan, the alignment is growing: "Preparing more than 50 million students with the knowledge and skills to succeed in college and careers is the greatest moral and economic challenge of our era" (Bush & Wise, 2010, p. 4).

> ### REFLECTION/STUDY QUESTION
>
> Has your school/community begun the discussion of what constitutes 21st century skills? How do your findings compare with EDUCATION CONNECTION's Center for 21st Century Skills crosswalk list?

Truth 2: Proper Preparation for the Digital Age Requires Digital Access

How Do We Achieve Fluency?

Agreeing with this truth requires only an application of common sense. The famous question "How do you get to Carnegie Hall?" has only one answer that works: practice. To gain fluency and understanding in any arena demands sustained work and feedback over many years. Want to be a good chef? You need to cook. Want to be a scratch golfer? You must practice and play—a lot. The same goes for reading, writing, public speaking, and any other skill-based pursuit.

This is the foundation of Truth 2: Adequate preparation for a 21st century digital work and learning environment demands that students have ready 1:1 access to technology and aligned instructional practices so that they may invest the time needed to become fluent users of these tools. The reality of teaching and learning for the 21st century is that to prepare students for an environment that is constantly changing and adapting, educators must be able to replicate or introduce them to learning experiences that prepare them for it. To be fluent with problem solving and adaptability, to be digitally literate adults, learners must practice and use these skills consistently over time.

This is not about the mechanical use of the devices themselves. Anyone who has seen a teen tackle a new phone or gadget that she has never touched before and immediately start playing with it, experimenting with it, and figuring out how it works knows this is true. Practical technology proficiency is easy for a generation raised in its midst. Fluency and understanding of how these tools are used appropriately for knowledge creation in a rigorous and accountable learning environment is an acquired talent that is rarely mastered without lots of practice.

The point of Truth 2 is that technology devices and 1:1 access to them is the platform on which the skills to thoughtfully solve problems in a digital academic environment are built. Just as you would never get in a car driven by someone who has learned to drive only by reading a manual, it would be equally misguided to think students—or their teachers, for that matter—who have predominately used static print texts as training for digital information processing would be ready for that challenge.

Living in One World, Learning in Another

And yet, for a variety of fiscal and cultural reasons, this is the model that the vast majority of public schools continue to employ today. We distribute books and paper and implore students to be ready to learn every day, but we ban or restrict the use of the devices they know they will need or use for the rest of their lives to do the exact same work. Fearing a loss of control, we create policies that lock down networks and access to information sources. If students are lucky, they get to spend a couple of periods a week in the computer lab, using a machine that is not their own, to do a little searching or to put the finishing touches on a project. In an average American public school setting, it is safe to say that as a matter of total time on task, the digital information tools that students need the most practice with are the ones that they collectively have the least access to.

If this seems too harsh, consider how we teach and assess what endures as the most tested of all expressive thinking skills: writing. Think of the gap between the way this skill is taught and assessed and the predominant methods under which it is applied. Students spend all of their recreational and personal writing time composing on a keyboard or voice-recognition device with ready editing capability. Additionally, it is virtually certain that every word a student will ever write for an important task in a value-added job in his lifetimes will be composed the same way.

But, when it comes to on-demand writing in school—or, more critically, the all-important time-limited assessment of responsive writing—what is the practice? Teachers introduce these assessments with phrases like, "Open your blue books and be sure you have three sharp pencils and a workable eraser before you start writing." With that, we begin critical assessments that can play a role in determining a student's future using a process that she will never use again once she leaves school. How many kids have we underestimated or labeled as poor writers due mainly to the fact that we do not give them a chance to demonstrate the skill through a process that is aligned with their primary compositional strategy? The way we assess writing now is more a reflection of a student's ability to use antiquated methods than it is a measure of his absolute writing potential given appropriate tools.

As we should expect, in multiple studies of writing testing, starting as early as a decade ago, students who were allowed to compose answers on computers consistently write longer and higher quality responses than those tested with paper and pencil (Russell & Plati, 2000). Would we ask a musician seeking to be an orchestra's first violin audition for that honor by playing the clarinet? Sure, the musical principles are the same, but the application is vastly different with the unfamiliar instrument. Asking students to regularly prove, in the context of our current high-stakes testing environment, their writing ability with one tool while we know they will and must use another seems fundamentally unfair.

As long as public schools remain primarily paper and textbook based, the gulf between the appropriateness of the preparation system we provide and the learning and work environment that our students will enter continues to grow. As the distance between these two worlds widens, the degree to which students question the credibility of the process will increase along with it. Once that skepticism reaches critical mass, you can shut the schoolhouse doors because the authenticity battle will have been lost. Without 1:1 access to the tools that form the foundation of 21st century learning and work, students cannot be properly prepared for life in this environment—and they know it. Facing Truth 2 is no less than a matter of survival for public schools.

REFLECTION/STUDY QUESTION

Can you think of other areas, subjects, or processes where the print/textbook instructional systems are out of alignment with the digital systems that predominate outside of the public school environment? How have you engaged your students or children in discussions about these gaps? If so, how do their responses inform your thinking about the urgency to make a public school transition to a digital learning environment? What would your community's reaction be to the goal of getting out of the textbook business within three years?

Truth 3: Continued Investment in Print Is a Waste

Once we accept the inevitability of Truths 1 and 2, what naturally follows is just logic. The goal is digital, the current state is print; if you want to move from one to the other, then further investment in the print-based system of instruction you want to leave behind is a waste. If the term *waste* seems too strong, consider what Jim Collins says in *Good to Great* (2001), where he demonstrates that in every organization seeking improvement, there will come a time when they have to "face the brutal truth." His point is that until we label and confront unaligned and misguided work for what it is, we will never have the strength or impetus to change it. When the facts show that performance is poor or your methods are ineffectual given your goal, you cannot put a shine on it and just hope it will get better. You have to look at the underlying reasons behind the data and act on the root causes. History is littered with extinct institutions that believed that their past successes guaranteed a bright future despite what the data told them as they were on their way down.

For schools, this means facing the reality that continued investment in a print educational infrastructure and the lack of sound transitional planning for a complete move to digital are ultimately counterproductive. If we want to prepare students for the 21st century, then the overriding strategic and resource-allocation goal for all public schools must be to create a system where all students have 1:1 access to the tools and instructional settings required for 21st century success. This conclusion makes good rational sense, and most educators understand it and would act on the notion if they could; they just don't see how getting to 1:1 is possible in the current budgetary climate.

The goal of a transition to 1:1 tempts us like a shiny lure. We can see what the potential of the instructional model is by looking toward the handful of districts, schools, and the one state (Maine) that have already found a way to jump across the gap between the print and digital worlds. Authors like Pamela Livingston have documented the successes of 1:1 efforts and provide sound guidance on what is required for success. Her book, *1-to-1 Learning: Laptop Programs That Work* was published by ISTE in 2006 and is now in its second edition (Livingston, 2009). Cathleen Norris and Elliot Soloway (2011) from the University of Michigan have written similarly about the success of 1:1 efforts using handheld devices as well. Effective programs in this realm always have clear goals; enough learning structure to provide guidance, along with the freedom to allow for the empowerment of learning; and good infrastructure support.

In my own experience, when exposed for the first time to the potential of a 1:1 21st century learning challenge, I have seen veteran teachers' enthusiasm for the profession reignited. I have watched students from every possible demographic work long hours, struggle and persevere, excel, and then speak with pride about their work as they shared it with others. We will explore these success stories and the lessons learned from them more deeply in Chapters 5 and 6. Suffice it to say at this point that the data are pretty clear: When designed and supported properly, a rigorous, problem/challenge/inquiry–based 1:1 instructional system is more aligned with the purpose, interest, and needs of a digital generation. Despite this clarity, it is at this point that the promise and desire to move to 1:1 usually gets stalled amid a myriad of frustrating barriers and dead ends.

Money, Money, Money—and Other Barriers

First, and unfortunately, there is the matter of money. In the current economic and school budget climate, even with consistently falling technology prices, it is hard for most educators to imagine that they will ever be able to finance a move to 1:1. Based on our traditional expectations, we know that if we are going to require or assign something in school, we have to provide every student with a copy. If we wanted to get to 1:1 using traditional notebook computers and this supply model, under the best conditions, that would cost $500 to $750 per student. With a school size of 752, this means it would cost at least half a million dollars to get 1:1 off the ground in an average American high school (National Center for Education Statistics, 2002). It is interesting that in some communities, the accumulated yearly cost of supporting print education is greater on a per-pupil basis than this device cost, but the challenge of coming up with the big chunk of money all at once prevents the consideration of the move to digital.

We will explore these figures in more detail in the next chapter, but let's assume at this point that these start-up costs are the main reason that many of the first 1:1 initiatives undertaken had to be supported by outside resources, began as classroom pilots, or had to be introduced one grade at a time. Today, it seems that for most districts, in a time when they struggle just to keep up with staffing and benefit costs, large one-time or multiyear start-up investments in technology seem impossibly out of reach. It is for all practical purposes a non-starter—"Sure, we would love to get to 1:1, but we can't afford it." End of story.

But what if a district could afford it? What if there was a combination of strategies that could be pieced together with only your current budget resources that would result in every student having her own digital device and ultimately enabling your district's transition to digital learning? Is that something you might be interested in learning more about?

This is the promise of *Digital Learning for All, Now*. Every district that is willing to think a little differently about resource allocation and instructional programming can afford the move to 1:1 learning, and the move can start today. It is a change process with two movements, however. First are the fiscal, policy, and technical changes (Chapters 2 and 3) that enable the acquisition of the technology. Next come the much more difficult professional adaptive changes required to shift goals, instruction, and assessment processes into alignment with 21st0century learning (Chapters 4, 5, and 6).

The good news is that the move to 1:1 is financially possible; we can get there from here. In the broadest sense, the key to the *Digital Learning for All, Now* financial strategy is the reinvestment of assets garnered through three different changes:

1. Leveraging crowdsourcing to supplement the districts hardware capability—in other words, letting students who want to, and can afford to, bring their own devices to school for use in an official school capacity

2. Saving money from the elimination or drastic reduction in the number of textbooks, copies, and printed material required for the educational enterprise

3. Savings realized by the elimination of redundant work caused by the current technology scarcity model employed in most districts

As Chapters 2 and 3 are each devoted to detailed descriptions of these first two changes, I want to explain the third, the end of the "scarcity model." Most businesses and organizations have made the transition from print to digital processes, and once they do, they rarely continue to replicate the original process in the presence of the new technology. For example, once a store starts using QuickBooks to track its finances, it probably does not keep a backup set of handwritten ledgers. It backs up the new processes data but does not run a duplicate print system, as the waste of such an endeavor is readily apparent.

In schools, because of our traditional one-size-fits-all ethic and egalitarian history, we assume that if everyone can't have access to something, then we must either not use it or buy it for all. So, no matter how much technology we purchase, if we do not achieve 100 percent coverage, we are obligated to provide a duplicate print system to ensure that no student is left without the basics. In teaching American history, for example, even though the class is going to go to the computer lab for three weeks in February to work on a project, the rest of the time, every student still needs a textbook. Bring on the 900-page, eight-pound, $100 textbook to guide them through their print-based learning journey.

The result is an overlap between print and digital instructional resources that creates a costly redundancy in educational systems. This is a wasteful overlap that schools cannot afford. In addition to the increased costs caused by the redundancy, because students so rarely have access to technology, design changes that take advantage of the growing pool of online instructional resources are restricted. The final result means lots of money spent on technology but very little learning gain acquired for the investment. This dynamic is described in Figure 1.4.

Figure 1.4   Technology Scarcity Model

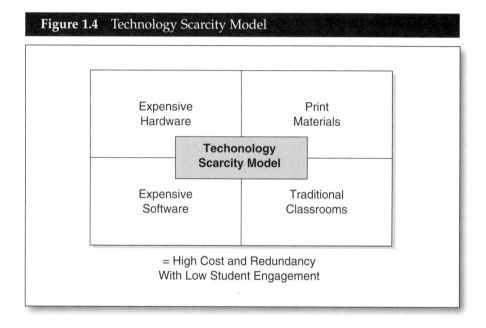

= High Cost and Redundancy
With Low Student Engagement

Once you are able to make design decisions based on an assumption of 1:1 access for all students, you immediately are free of the expensive redundancies that shackle the school budget in the scarcity model. You now have a number of different options within your reach that allow you to save additional money. These include the elimination of reliance on print materials, the reduction of copies, increased flexibility in transportation and facilities use, and many more. But as we know, it's about more than just money. With a 1:1 technology access model, the instructional environment can be redesigned to be more responsive to the needs of the generation of learners you are serving. Additionally, as we will explore more completely in Chapter 5, you have the ability to engage and empower learners through the technology in ways that print simply cannot duplicate. This access model is described in the next figure.

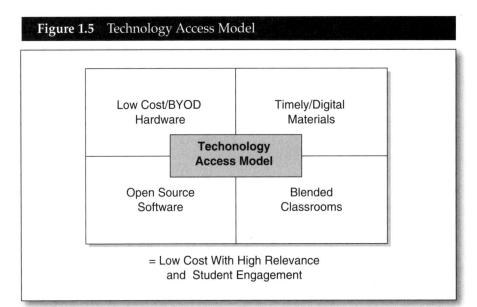

Figure 1.5   Technology Access Model

This approach can work, it does work, and more and more districts are starting the journey to make it so. The first step is getting started on the hardware problem. As mentioned earlier, when we have traditionally approached this issue, we have started the conversation with the question, "How can we afford to buy every student a device that is appropriate for full participation in a digital learning environment?" Most of the answers to this question are predictably depressing. What happens, however, when we change the question to "How can we ensure that every student has a device that is appropriate for full participation in a digital learning environment?" and avoid the assumption that schools have to be the sole provider of those devices? When it is put this way, one of the answers can be, "Let's let them bring their own." Chapter 2 will explore in detail the coming revolution that is Bring Your Own Device, or BYOD.

REFLECTION/STUDY QUESTION

What areas of waste and redundancy do you see between the print and digital systems at work in your district/school? What work and costs could be eliminated, combined, or saved if you knew that every student and home would have 24/7 access a digital device?

CHAPTER SUMMARY

In this first chapter, we have explored the history of technology's advance and its impact on our culture and, ultimately, on our schools. With that as context, we then walked through three indisputable truths that frame the rationale behind this book: (1) that the future of learning and works is digital, (2) that students need access to digital learning to become fluent, and finally, (3) that print investments are counter to the mission of effective preparation for students in a digital age. We know we need to get to a 1:1 instructional model, but so far, we just have not had the financial resources to make that happen on a large scale. This is why an affordable solution to bridge the gap between print and digital is such an exciting possibility. BYOD is that solution, and Chapter 2 is all about how to make it work.

PART II

Getting to 1:1

2

BYOD

Crowdsourcing Hardware and Closing the Equity Gap

An Introduction to Bring Your Own Device

As noted in the first chapter, even when per-pupil costs for digital devices are lower than the accumulated print costs of public school education, the challenge of finding the up-front money to purchase enough devices to make 1:1 work prevents districts from making the move. In the current financial climate, proposals that increase the bottom line, even if only temporarily, face likely doom.

A different approach is needed. Bring Your Own Device, or BYOD, is a strategy where districts encourage students to bring their own Internet-capable devices to school and to use them as the primary platforms for learning. In BYOD practice, a district creates a minimum technology device standard and then invites any student who has a device that meets that standard to bring it and use it in school. These device standards could be as simple as defining wireless access capability, minimum screen size, and browser support criteria (type, version, media support). According to the Pew Internet & American Life Project (2009), between 70 percent and 80 percent of the American student population already has a device that meets a similar standard.

With that as a foundation, imagine what the total percentage of ready users would be if families were told that if they purchased a similar device, their sons or daughters would be able to use it in schools? When the vast majority of your students come to school with a learning-capable device in hand, districts can then redeploy the money saved from the strategies described in Chapter 3 to purchase selected devices for those students who either cannot afford or do not want to provide one of their own.

This combination of resources is what closes the financing gap and enables the achievement of a 1:1 ratio. Once this is achieved, instructional systems can then be realigned with an assumption of digital access. This 100 percent coverage will unlock other savings throughout the business of the district as well as it enables the dismantling of parallel print systems that may no longer be needed now that all students have access to digital resources.

BYOD requires thoughtful management, but, when facilitated properly, it is the key to making 1:1 a reality in any public school district. With students bringing their own devices and districts providing only for those that cannot provide for themselves, 1:1 is within the immediate reach of every district. Quite simply, it is the public schools' last best chance to make the needed immediate leap to digital learning environments.

Three Trends That Make BYOD Possible

BYOD is in its infancy and early adoption phase because technology limitations had made it an impractical consideration. Adequate equipment was too expensive to acquire, needed software was costly and required large hard drives and processing power to run, and the change imperative was less urgent. Combined, these factors became a formidable barrier and meant that if a district wanted to move to 1:1, the only option was to write a really big check and buy every student an appropriate device. This works if it can be afforded, but the measly number of districts who are currently using 1:1 with all of their students is testament to the tiny percentage that could spend the required resources to make that happen. Recently, three major trends have enabled the viability of the BYOD option.

Trend 1: Lighter, Faster, Smaller, Cheaper

First among these trends is the ongoing benefit of Moore's Law. As described in Chapter 1, this is the common-knowledge term that describes the development of relentlessly greater functionality within the device market without corresponding increases in price (Intel, 2005).

Since the mid-1980s, anyone who has purchased technology has experienced this phenomenon. The functionality of a desktop that cost $5,000 in 1990 can now be carried around in your pocket. And amazingly, that $300 portable device will actually do tasks that the desktop never dreamed of doing. My first home computer, purchased in 1987, was little more than a gray-scale word processor in a Macintosh case and cost $4,300. My iPhone, by comparison, in addition to being a phone and Internet-access device, will also do everything from analyze student performance data and identify actual mountain peak elevations through the viewfinder, to listen to me and respond when I talk, and it costs only 10 percent of that original Apple product.

Even though consumers are sometimes flustered by the relentlessness of this phenomenon, the process in general benefits everyone. The only downside is that sinking feeling a person gets when just months after purchasing a device, a newer model becomes available and the original is worth half of what was paid. Happily, as equipment has become more functional and less costly, the potential expense of running a digital school system has decreased significantly.

Consider these numbers. When trying to finance the shift to a digital system, one key metric is per-pupil expense for supporting instruction. As I will explain in detail in Chapter 3, this figure can be determined by adding up all of the costs associated with support of print instruction. Textbooks, materials, copies—all of these components figure in identifying a per-pupil instructional cost. On average, over the course of a four-year high school stay, these per-pupil numbers are in the annual range of $135 to $250.

REFLECTION/STUDY QUESTION

Do you know what your current per-pupil instructional support number is? Without this data, you will not be able to determine the fiscal viability of 1:1 or BYOD. Using the textbook data from Chapter 2 as a start, itemize and identify the total annual per-pupil cost of supporting instruction in your current configuration. Is it higher than you thought?

For comparison, when moving to digital services, if one uses a traditional laptop configuration from as recently as early 2008, per-pupil estimates for providing these devices ranged from $900 to

$1,500. This is what it used to cost for most laptop units and the associated software licenses for the basic programs required. At the time of this book's publication, entry-level MacBook Pros started at a retail price of $1,199.

NUMBERS WARNING

Readers should be aware that the price reference points used in *Digital Learning for All, Now* are from November 2011. Given what we know about technology pricing, it is my expectation that at the time of reading, these will have shifted lower. Specific device and price references are used to illustrate the point; use the logic and formula to make your own determinations in the market you are in today. Inevitably, the transition to 1:1 will be *easier* as time goes on because prices will continue to fall.

According to the National Center for Education Statistics (2002), the average high school in the United States has 752 students. Taking a median price of $1,200 per unit, prior to 2008, it would cost an average size high school $902,440 to move all instruction to 1:1. No matter what would be saved by not buying textbooks, it would never be enough to make the per-pupil cost of computers comparable with print. At these prices, boards of education were hard-pressed to make the change to digital because, even though it was instructionally the right thing to do, it was clearly going to drive up the cost of running the education enterprise. Because of the cost, technology for students is considered a luxury item.

This is no longer true. In current markets, there is an entirely new generation of devices that do much of what their more expensive predecessors did at a fraction of the cost. For example, a new generation of highly functional smaller laptop devices generically called netbooks and similar devices like Android-based tablets are designed to take advantage of the growth of cloud-based applications and cost about a third of what traditional laptops do. These devices can do most of what their more expensive and larger laptop cousins will, and as cloud resources grow, their functionality grows as well.

Classrooms built around these devices can be fully digital with complete access to the Internet and digital materials, eliminating the need for print materials. They can also run Internet-based applications like YouTube, Google Maps, or Blogster. Netbook models from major manufacturers like Dell and HP start at a retail price of just over $250. Google makes a similar device called a Chromebook named after its Internet browser. Entry-level Android tablets also start around $200. Just using an entry-level netbook as a starting price point, that would drop the cost of buying every student a device at the average high school from the 2008 estimate of $902,440 to a current price of $188,000.

It is important to note that netbooks are not suggested here as the only viable solution to support a BYOD effort. There are a number of devices and options that will do what netbooks do and they are all possibilities. Tablets, smartphones—the technology changes all of the time, and there will be new options that arrive to market while this book is in production. The point is that every district and individual should make their own device selections based on their plans, preferences, and resources. The consideration here is a value equation based on price, utility, and affordability. Of course, a MacBook Pro does more than a netbook, and it would be great if every student could have one. But the reality is that most districts cannot afford it when taking that device to scale. A $200 netbook or similar device that can facilitate the move to digital today is a better choice than waiting indefinitely for something better to come along.

Trend 2: The Browser and the Price Benefit of Open Source

This downward hardware price movement is assisted by the open-source and cloud-based software trends that will be described fully in Chapter 3. Built into the per-unit cost of every PC or Mac are substantial software costs.

A traditional performance laptop's $1,200 price tag is typically 80 percent for hardware and 20 percent for license fees for software. That $1,200 laptop would really cost only $960 if it came with just the hardware. But add the Windows or Mac operating system, Microsoft Office, and other proprietary programs and the price balloons to what we have come to expect as the final tally. So ingrained and profitable is this practice, it is often difficult to order machines without much of this software installed. All machines come with proprietary operating systems by default because manufacturers and software companies make money on every unit they sell. Add Microsoft Office or other software choice options that are built into the design process queue and watch that price go up, up, and away.

It's hard to imagine buying a computer without installed software, but it can be done and can save a lot of money. Knowing how to get a blank machine to boot with Linux or another open-source operating system can get a buyer started without the expense of the proprietary operating system. Some who try this approach get resistance from manufacturers, but schools that buy in bulk have some purchasing leverage. A single consumer or district asking Dell to sell her a clean netbook for $200 instead of $250 is going to be annoyance. A request for 5,000 royalty-free machines by a purchasing consortium has a better chance of succeeding.

It is ironic that many states, including my own, Connecticut, have purchasing consortia originally designed to save money on proprietary licenses and traditional hardware. Regardless of the targeted purchase, it does reduce prices. This has been demonstrated by the state of Maine, which, through many years of buying Apple laptops, has succeeded in getting the per-unit price down to about 50 percent of retail (J. Mao, personal communication, April 26, 2011). This same purchasing power could be combined to buy BYOD and open-source supported hardware in a way that avoids the need for proprietary software. Also, truly enterprising districts can have machines built with component parts for fractions of what is available through huge manufacturers. Either way, the goal should be to purchase hardware-only configurations that will then allow the district to take advantage of the open-source software marketplace.

If a district were to use a basic tablet or purchase license-free netbooks that had no software except those from sources that were open, the per-unit cost could be reduced to around $200. With cost contained at $200 per unit, the price of a complete conversion to digital at our average high school would now be down from nearly $1 million to $150,400.

While this is a significant reduction, even if this number could be afforded, there will be those who argue that these "low end" devices are not functional enough to justify the price. There are times when a "you get what you pay for" attitude is justified. Fortunately, if districts are careful and do their homework, purchasing technology does not always have to be one of those times.

REFLECTION/STUDY QUESTION

Have you or any of the adults in key leadership positions in your district ever used a device that depended on open-source software? If not, explore the reasons or concerns that have prevented that experience. Would you/they be willing to have a technician or a knowledgeable student reformat a district laptop to run this type of configuration so it could be demystified and understanding increased?

Not "Bare Bones" Anymore

It is a common misconception that open-source devices that run without proprietary software are barren of functional programs that support teaching and learning and could never actually support a rich instructional program. Recent developments of Internet and cloud-based solutions have turned this perception around. The emergence of cloud-based computing has put the development focus of mainstream solutions squarely on the browser.

Through it, one can run Google Docs, a word processor that not only is free but also offers collaboration and sharing tools that are superior to software that requires licenses. How about using Moodle, a course creation and delivery platform that is free and versatile enough to support courses for learners from kindergarten through graduate school? We have used Moodle in our Center for 21st Century Skills as our primary learning platform since 2005. All these programs and more are driven through the browser. In focusing on the browser, developers have identified the portal that offers the greatest access to the highest number of users. If a company wants consumers to use their service, it is in their best interest to make it as accessible as possible, and the browser works because any device that runs a browser can access these programs for free—phones, tablets, PCs, Macs, netbooks, anything.

This browser focus is making hardware selection a less stressful exercise. It used to be that creating hardware standards was a far more complex exercise because involved in that calculation were a myriad of variables: what programs needed to run, how much RAM was required, what were the minimum processing speeds required—and the list goes on. This is why past purchasing behaviors in districts were always guided by a specific device choice. "We buy only Dell Dimension 9200s" or similar statements were common because the district tech staff knew that these machines would do what was needed. Standardizing hardware purchases also simplified support functions.

Embrace Device Agnosticism

But, if a district's main concern is only to run the browser, then all the district needs to do is get a device that will do that. A variety of devices will meet this need, and any or all are decent options depending on the environment and planned uses. In a browser-focused world, Amazon's Kindle Fire, other Android-based tablets, older generation iPads, the iPod Touch, any Android phone, the Motorola

Zoom, or anything else that will run a browser can potentially get the job done. This book was composed in part on an iPhone, an iPad, a five-year-old Dell Dimension 9200 desktop, a Dell Inspiron laptop, and a new Apple MacBook Air. The device choice is irrelevant if it functions well enough to accomplish the task at hand. Districts should work with their tech staff to determine which devices work best for the most students and make purchase decisions based on the results (see Figure 2.1).

Figure 2.1   Device Feature Comparison Chart

Device	Per Unit Cost	Capacity	Add/Dis
Cell Phone			
Smart Phone			
Tablet/Pad			
Netbook			
Classmate/ Chromebook			
Laptop			

To download an electronic version of this table so you can adapt it and use it in your own school community, go to **http://www.digitallearningforallnow .com,** click on the Digital Resources button, select the appropriate chapter from the drop-down menu, and enter the password **D L F A N** (all uppercase). In this area, you will find all of the digital resources presented in the book and more.

Whichever hardware choice is made, the flexibility created by browser access is the most important purchasing criterion when considering *Digital Learning for All, Now* strategies. The market moves too quickly, and the technology future is too uncertain. Going all-in on any one device is always risky, as it is a certainty that within a year or two at the most, there will be an entirely new generation of the same product that does more, costs less, and renders the current device as just another choice. With a BYOD device strategy that is elastic and tied to the browser, teachers have a more adaptable platform to work with. By focusing on the browser, a district greatly expands the flexibility of device application and increases the number of options that can help students be successful. The browser is as close to a constant as there is in a digital age. Devices that can get a student to the browser will have longer practical lives than devices that cannot.

So, with this open-source browser focus in mind, let's return our attention to the netbook example. Will these $200 devices do everything? No, they won't, is the direct answer. But as we will see in Chapter 3 in the exploration of open-source software, they don't have to do everything to be useful and to be a good value. The same 90/10 value equation we will use to determine the value of open-source software applies here in the hardware domain as well. If a purchased product will do 90 percent of the functions of a device that costs 70 percent more per unit, is that increased price worth the last 10 percent of the device's functionality? A MacBook starts at $999 and a netbook can be purchased for $200. Admittedly, the MacBook will run programs (Garage Band) that the netbook or a small-scale device like a Chromebook will not, but the netbook would allow the student to access all of the course materials in the general digital curriculum. Is having access to a cool media program worth another $799 per unit?

Figure 2.2 The 90/10 Value Equation

The 90/10
Value Equation

If the answer makes the difference between being able to afford the move to 1:1 and having to wait indefinitely, district leaders have to say, "No, it is not worth the price." To reiterate, these are not bare-bones devices that will only load a textbook or do word processing. Rather, these are highly functional devices that can be loaded with the Edubuntu Linux operating system, Open Office or Google Docs for Office type functions, the Firefox browser to provide access to anything web based, and basically everything a student would need to participate in an instructional environment designed around the browser.

There will always be specialty functions that these browser-focused devices cannot perform. For example, a netbook's small hard drive and processor are not appropriate for 3D modeling or Computer Assisted Design (CAD) functions. Digital music production or video editing is simply not practical on a small screen and keyboard. Some online testing contexts require secure terminals and specific refresh rates. These are advanced or particular functions that computer labs should be for. Instead of these labs being the place where students get their only exposure to working in a digital environment two or three times a week, they can be converted into specialty use areas where higher performing desktops can run programs that student's everyday-use, browser-focused devices will not.

Imagine a high school where all students have the devices they need to do their daily tasks and learning work, and they carry that device with them at all times. At various points in the day or year, when classes with specific high-function needs occur, they go to a lab that has the necessary equipment. All students do not need a work station capable of running a CAD program or rendering a digital animation, so districts should provide enough for small groups to do these tasks but should not try to finance that capacity overreach for all. All students do, however, need access to the Internet and to be able to use the browser and cloud as a platform to develop 21st century skills. This is the foundation of navigating the complexity of the information age. All they need is a device to do that, and it need not be unaffordable.

REFLECTION/STUDY QUESTION

What would an "Open Phone Test" look like, and does the prospect of having such an event make you or your staff nervous? If so, why? Explore these concerns—they are critical to understanding how ingrained a print mindset is in your instructional culture and what challenges are present in a move to 1:1.

Do the Math!

Returning to the budget, as previously stated, with an open-source device price contained at around $200 per unit, the cost of a complete conversion to digital at our average high school is now down to $150,400. This figure is manageable when compared to the near million-dollar hurdle of buying a device for every student, but it is probably still more than most districts have readily available in their budgets.

Enter BYOD. Once again, using an average community as a reference point, if one were to use a $200 entry purchasing price point and invite students to bring their own Internet-ready equipment to school, experience shows that at least 75 percent of the students would do so. This can be predicted based on what current BYOD districts have experienced and what can be inferred from current usage statistics regarding phones and Internet access in American homes (Harris Interactive, 2008).

In every community, many students already have an Internet-ready device that would accomplish this goal, and many more would go out and get one, either of their own selection or from a district purchasing pool if they had the opportunity to do so. Using 75 percent of the student body as self-providing as a general reference, imagine what this means for the cost of digital conversion. A district now needs only to provide those $200 netbooks for 25 percent of the student body, or just 188 students. Now, the cost of 1:1 conversion is down to $37,600.

As will be demonstrated in Chapter 3, the data shows when districts stop buying textbooks and licensed software in a conversion to open source, they save enough money to cover the cost of those netbooks with plenty to spare. I work with a small K–6 district in the northwestern corner of Connecticut that identified nearly $45,000 when district staff examined the cost of supporting print instruction in their 2011–2012 budget. If an economically conservative K–6 district can do it, anyone can. Allowing redirected savings to cover access just for those who need it is how BYOD makes 1:1 affordable for everyone.

Earlier, it was suggested that per-pupil print support expenditure was between $135 and $250 annually for a student attending a four-year high school. Using a $200 netbook and 75 percent self-provision estimate, the per-pupil instructional support number in the reference average school of 752 students would be well below that annual print-support figure through those student's careers, perhaps as low as $50. What happens when districts start to understand that improving the instructional environment can cost less than half per pupil than the current system? BYOD will quickly go from its current vanguard/ experimental status to something that all districts will consider implementing.

Trend 3: Customize or Perish

From these examples, it is easy to see how decreasing hardware costs and the growth of the browser enable a shift to BYOD. The third trend that supports this move has its roots in technology but manifests itself culturally. This is the development of technology-enabled customization that has swept over the consumer culture. It is the "have it my way" outlook that has kicked "one size fits all" to the curbside. Any consumer-focused business that does not leverage the power of technology to meet the particular needs of its individual patrons is exposed to failure in this environment.

Suppliers remember wistfully the simpler times when a take-it-or-leave-it attitude was prevalent. Best exemplified by the Henry Ford–produced Model T, every purchaser knew he could have any color he wanted—as long as it was black. Today, there is choice in every purchasing decision. Order a regular cup of coffee? How about a half-caf, mocha, nonfat latte with extra shots? Consumers can design their own burgers, shoes, sneakers, clothes, car options—everything.

Even within the compressed history of computer purchasing, the same trends are evident. There were no options in the first wave of Macs and PCs. Grab the box off the shelf and plug it in. Beige or black plastic was considered choice in the early 1980s. Today, every computer manufacturer has a webpage that allows consumers to design their own machines from the chassis up. Every option is possible; all it takes is money.

This extends beyond the hardware. The explosion the "app ecosystem" is another example of this. Even if two people purchased the same phone, with 500,000 different applications available, every one of the millions of iPhone or Android phones sold are set up and customized to meet the whims and preferences of the owner. Developers crank these applications out in astonishing numbers, sending them to market daily. As anyone who has visited the Apple, Android, or Blackberry App markets can attest, the options are always changing, and prices are low. The average price of an iPhone application is under $2 (Zibreg, 2011).

This environment is an individualists dream. In the early 21st century, consumers believe that customization is near birthright. Why then would anyone believe that students would want to have the same copy of anything when all around them customization is the expectation? Every student is unique and would probably approach things differently if she had the chance to do so. Taking advantage of personalization and custom setup options is a teen expectation when it comes to technology.

REFLECTION/STUDY QUESTION

What role does ownership and control play in determining a learner's willingness to engage meaningfully in the process of learning? Think of your own most powerful learning experiences in either a school or personal setting. How did your own investment in those settings drive the meaning that came from them?

BYOD in Industry

This is exactly the pressure that has brought industry, as it has in so many other areas, to lead education to be the first to begin to embrace BYOD. This is particularly ironic as the public perception is always that industry has access to all the capital it needs, so why would companies take on the added perceived network-security risks of BYOD if they did not really need to? The answer is that their employees overwhelmingly want to be able to use their own phones and set them up the way that they want them rather than be chained to the traditional boring office phone or locked-down Blackberry that the industrial IT department has provided.

As security concerns have been overcome, industry has come to see this as a win-win situation. The business saves money on equipment, and the employee gets to have his phone outfitted the way he wants. This trend has extended to phone service as well. There are now a variety of providers, like BroadVoice, that let consumers use their own phones on stand-alone VoIP (voice Internet protocol) networks. This avoids lengthy service contracts and just allows users to buy and sell their own phones and use whatever device they want on the common network.

Own Your Own Learning

BYOD works similarly in schools. In addition to its financial benefits, BYOD allows students to take ownership of their equipment choices and customize their own work environments. BYOD districts encourage students to personalize their own machines—even those that the district provides. This ownership and customized setup facilitates the deepening of student engagement that is a major goal of moving to a 1:1 environment. One of the other benefits of this student ownership dynamic is a much lower than predicted damage and loss rate for machines in student possession. We will look at this issue more closely in Chapter 4, but suffice it to say that when students control their own devices, they take care of them, and districts can manage with buffer pools of less than 5 percent of their total device population.

Decreasing hardware costs, the development of the browser, and the drive for customization have all helped to combine to make BYOD a viable strategy to help make the transition to 1:1. The numbers work; by pursuing BYOD a district can absolutely make the change and bring universal digital instructional practices to every learner. Because BYOD is a fairly new idea that challenges some long-held practices, however, there are issues that need to be considered as communities consider pursuing it.

Implementation Challenges for BYOD

Depending on the community, first reactions to a proposed BYOD strategy can be initially critical. Regardless of the solid rationale behind it, district leaders are wise to remember that the movement from print to digital represents the biggest structural change in public education since the creation of the high school. I have seen superintendents launch BYOD efforts certain of the rightness of the cause only to be blindsided by community resistance to the shift. This is why from the earliest inkling of a district thinking of moving in this direction, engaging the board, parents, staff, and general community in a dialogue about the motivations and advantages of BYOD and 1:1 learning is a must. Hold meetings, listen to the issues, and respond thoughtfully. Without this process, misinformation and surprises will inevitably complicate your efforts to make this transition.

Such is the fate of practices that stretch boundaries and appear to be novel in a school setting. While the entirety of Chapter 4 is focused on the broad barriers related to perception and policy involved in a movement to 1:1, the objections to BYOD are specific. These responses generally can be categorized in three ways: 1) philosophical objections—these come from constituents that believe that it is the moral obligation of towns and schools to provide what is needed for a free and adequate public education; 2) equity concerns—if one student has an expensive piece of equipment that her rich parents purchased, she has an advantage over a student who can't afford that model and has to make do with the district-purchased machine; 3) security concerns—BYOD can be particularly stressful on parents and IT departments. First, some moms and dads will envision their children freely roaming the Internet, and then your technology staff will foresee the nightmare of hundreds of strange devices joining their fragile network infrastructures. While some of these issues are real and others are based on perception, either way, dealing with them effectively will mean the difference between success and failure of a BYOD installation.

Challenge 1: The District Should Pay

The first challenges to BYOD are based on the underlying belief that every community should provide all of what is needed for students to be properly educated. These are public schools; the public should provide what is needed. Unfortunately, even if there was agreement on this general principle, it has become painfully obvious in recent years that public school districts have consistently not lived up to this ideal.

Over the last two decades, the pressure of the school budget process has increased dramatically. Primarily driven by salary and benefit costs, the entire budget-passing ritual is one too often marked by tension and intense scrutiny. The result of this grind has been a slow bleeding of resources from nearly every instructional area. There rarely is money to do anything related to program improvement, and budget battles to maintain status quo services are the rule, not the exception.

Even if a move to 1:1 were an agreed-on priority, without the benefit of crowdsourcing the equipment through BYOD, the chances of it happening in this environment are slim. BYOD is critical because, given today's fiscal hardships at the national, state, and local levels, it is the only readily available strategy that can realistically overcome the huge fiscal barriers to implementing a 1:1 strategy. The laudable philosophical belief that all districts *should* pay for every student to have a device is made irrelevant by the current fiscal reality that most districts *cannot*, or *will not*, be able to allocate the funds to do so.

Not a New Precedent

A related financial angle arises when constituents object to implementing a BYOD strategy by saying that BYOD inappropriately shifts the responsibility for providing a free and public education only to the households who use it. This perspective holds that having only students' families bear the brunt of this purchase is wrong, that public schools are for all of the public and should therefore be supported by the entire community. Similar arguments are raised frequently when taxpayers object to having their tax dollars go to support programs that they do not support.

This principle of shared community responsibility is deeply and legitimately held and has passionate advocates who argue that it represents a failure of the public to meet its obligations to today's youth. This is a position that must be respected. Unfortunately, adhering to this position puts districts in an impossible bind. As just mentioned, depending on the local laws, school boards sometimes lack taxing authority and so have no options if they cannot get budgets passed. When faced with insufficient or declining revenues and a concurrent demand to buy equipment for 1:1, the only alternative is a massive layoff to save the money needed to finance the purchase. Trading technology for good teachers, no matter what the proposed use, is a bad bargain. Districts have nowhere to turn except to the all-too-common "well, we can always put it in next year's budget" strategy. Then the next year, the same scenarios play out again, and print reigns for another generation of students.

Another aspect of this "burden shift" argument is a warning that BYOD is somehow setting a new or first-time-ever precedent of placing the onus just on families with students in school. Those that would forward this argument need to remember two important points. First, in all BYOD districts, families who for any reason state that they cannot afford to participate must and should be granted waivers and provided with a district-purchased device with no questions asked. This waiver process is a practice that has a long history and is well established in most communities in any circumstance where an additional fee or resource for participation in school events is required. In my own district, this happens regularly for field trips, sports-participation fees, and specialty-program participation.

Second, anyone who believes that current district budgets supply all that children need for a free and adequate education have not been paying attention to the last twenty years of public school financing. Slowly and steadily, as local budget pressures have increased, the move to transfer some of the cost of instructional support to homes with children in schools has been under way. In my hometown, and many others, this process begins in kindergarten. Every summer, tucked into the letter that announces a child's teacher assignment is the official list of supplies that each child is expected to bring on the first day of school.

Included are all of the small things that parents used to assume the school would supply but are now the responsibility of the home. Pencils, paper, rulers, markers, book covers, and even sticky notes. It seems like small stuff, but taken together, our family's average contribution was easily $100 to $200 a year. Once the high school grades arrive, the stakes get much higher. Remember the Texas Instruments Graphing Calculators that are required for Algebra? That item cost my family $118 three times over (one for each of two boys plus one replacement). In many ways, BYOD is nothing more than the next logical step of having children come to school prepared for learning. In the 21st century, a netbook, tablet, or laptop is an integral part of that preparation. When compared to what all of the print-support supplies cost, at $200 per unit, it really is not that much more than families are used to paying right now.

In an era when every dime that the district spends is scrutinized, there has to be recognition that BYOD is fundamentally a smarter approach to resource provision in public schools. Many of these devices have already been purchased and are already sitting in homes anyway. As such, BYOD is just leveraging a resource that already exists but is underutilized for learning. As mentioned earlier, in BYOD communities, there are three categories of owner: those who have it already, those that will go out and get it, and finally, those who cannot afford it. It is those students who come from homes that fall into this third category that give rise to the equity concerns related to BYOD.

REFLECTION/STUDY QUESTION

To what degree has your district already shifted the burden of the daily educational enterprise to families? Do you currently ask parents to supply materials or tuition-type activity payments to support the educational process?

Challenge 2: It's About Equity

The print-capacity model that has dominated public schools from the beginning dictates that for every text assigned to students, the school is expected to provide identical copies to ensure equity. Using the *American Experience* to teach U.S. History to juniors? Your high school better have enough copies of that text to distribute to every student. The same goes for all texts in every other class as well. It should be a quaint memory, but it is still the case today that the book closet is the focus of instructional resource distribution in most public high schools.

In a print model, if two students have identical copies of the same book, other than the names of formerly cool students who were listed on the "This book belongs to" label, they were said to have equal and equitable access to the resource. The argument against BYOD is that if 75 percent of students are bringing their own technology, then the school introduces inequality in opportunity and unfair advantage by allowing wealthier students to potentially bring better technology to school than their peers.

In an earlier era, when the size and power of the CPU was the primary determinant of how much functionality was available to the user, this would be a legitimate criticism. One needs to keep in mind the developments that will be discussed in Chapter 3, along with the preceding discussion. The focus of 1:1 can effectively be built around the browser and the cloud, two windows of resource provision easily connectable with a wide variety of devices.

If an instructional environment is crafted around these tools, any device that accesses the Internet through a browser is going to be able to function effectively. This significantly reduces the disparity in the operational functionality among different devices. A top-of-the-line, Quad-Core powered, high-definition gaming laptop that costs thousands of dollars runs a browser displaying the same content in the same way as the $200 netbook described earlier.

Consider the print analogy. If a student were to get a textbook with only the even numbered chapters and have to compete with wealthier students who could afford both odd and even, the inequity of that situation would be obvious and unacceptable. But what if the only difference in the books were the cover art? If all of the contents inside were all exactly the same, does that change the quality of the learner's interaction with the content? If accepting alternative covers meant the difference between being able to have everyone read the book or not having the book at all, would a district make that choice and work to help people understand what was going on?

REFLECTION/STUDY QUESTION

To what level is equity for all students an explicitly expressed value in your community? Has equity and ensuring that all students have appropriate access and learning experiences to prepare them for the future been part of the public discourse in your community? Why has this been, or not been, the case?

The Kids Already Get It

Additionally, it is not like students do not already experience similar differences. According to the website *Pew Internet & American Life Project*, four out of give teens already carry a wireless device (Lenhart, Purchell, Smith, & Zickhur, 2010). All these devices are different, and students are used to this variety. The same is true with technology in the home. Students do not expect to see the same desktop, laptop, or television in their friends' homes. They understand choice, and managing the differences between nonstandard devices in a school does not seem like a barrier to end users at all. If one were to ask students if they would support BYOD if it hastened the arrival of technology at their schools, "yes" would probably be a resounding reply.

If there are any doubts, consider that according to the Speak Up 2010 survey, 67 percent of parents say they would buy an Internet device for their children to use if the school allowed it (Project Tomorrow, 2011). If this is what mom and dad think, one can just imagine what the kids themselves want. In Alvarado, Texas, a district with over 70 percent of their students on free and reduced lunch, nearly all of their population was able to produce a device that was capable of Internet access and that met the district's specifications (Berger, 2011).

Equity decisions are easy when they are theoretical and one sided. They are more difficult on the margins. If a district knew that by managing a few superficial differences, it could open the door to 1:1 access for all children, would it still stand on principle and say, "No, that is OK, it is fairer for students if we wait." If that is the answer, I will need to follow up and ask, how long are they willing to wait, and what exactly are they waiting for?

A New Achievement Gap

When examined through this lens, there is a powerful equity argument that favors the BYOD solution. In terms of adequate preparation for the 21st century as described in Chapter 1, those at the greatest disadvantage in today's public schools are those children without private access to technology and 21st century learning environments at home. Even though it might not be under ideal teaching and learning conditions, students in properly resourced homes at least have some access to information-age tools. At home, with access to these tools, they will use them to support their schoolwork or just to have fun and socialize. In the end, time spent in this environment is a form of preparation for the world beyond school in itself.

Students without this kind of ready access at home must depend on the meager scraps of time they get in the scarcity model provided at school. A period in the computer lab during library media classes or maybe a week spent on a unit or project if their teacher has the initiative to sign up for the laptop cart. These interactions are not systemic, they are not adequate, and they are quickly becoming as big a source of achievement gap concern as the more traditional print exposure deficits that reading teachers have been talking about for years.

Much has been written about the current reading level achievement gap between socioeconomic classes. In the debate about causation, significant weight is given to the time advantage given to wealthier children because of their early exposure to print-rich environments in the home. A child who starts kindergarten and has been read to for 2,000 hours has a significant advantage over a child that has never seen a printed page.

If school districts do nothing but wait and hope that someday they might be able to buy all students an appropriate Internet device, the skill gap in navigating this world between those that have access to it already and those that do not will continue to grow. There is already evidence to suggest that this gap already exists (Gutnick, Robb, Takeuchi, & Kotler, 2010, p. 22). Soon, with the advent of the Smarter Balance Assessment Consortium's planned partial online assessment in 2014–2015 of the new Common Core State Standards, this gap will become even more apparent as children with a higher level of comfort with the technology will certainly outperform those without similar skills (State of Washington Office of the Superintendent of Public Instruction, 2011). The longer we wait until a truly 1:1 environment is established at school, the greater the chance that this same print access achievement gap mistake will be repeated for future generations in the context of digital resources.

Worrying that children will somehow be harmed by using different devices in the classroom seems a smaller risk then the complete lack of access this well-intentioned objection would create. In the end, all that this "wait until we can afford to do it right" approach accomplishes is to deny the very students who need access the most from experiencing the teaching and learning practices best suited to prepare them for their futures.

Challenge 3: Networks, Capacity, and Security

The final area of concern that needs to be addressed in a move to BYOD is a series of important, but ultimately solvable, technology and security problems. First among these are security and network capacity issues. The good news is that nobody reading these words and thinking of going to 1:1 through BYOD will be the first to attempt it. Many enterprise and school-district solutions are readily available for the myriad of "what ifs" and possible problems that can crop up when districts start heading down this path. A key is to involve technology staff early and to set the mindset for positively moving forward properly and early.

A colleague of mine who was then an interim superintendent in an affluent Connecticut suburb had the right idea when he was wrestling with his IT staff in the spring of 2010. As a group, they were resisting the idea of making wireless access points available in their high school, citing network and security issues. After several planning sessions in which he was working to react to roadblocks and challenges raised by staff about why this was a bad idea technologically, he shifted the focus. Instead of being on the defensive, he stated simply, "Listen, you need to stop telling me all the reasons why this won't work and start talking to me about what we need to do to make it work." By putting the emphasis on moving forward together, the dialogue transitioned to a collaborative problem-solving tone and the job was done.

REFLECTION/STUDY QUESTION

What is the dominant tone in your technology use/support culture: protection or promotion? Regardless of the answer, do you believe this tone is set by the district-level leadership or by those in the IT department who bear the first-level responsibility for the technology itself?

Making It Happen: Attitude Makes a Difference

The preceding anecdote illustrates an important point regarding the changing roles of IT staff in a BYOD district. Folks that see their roles only through the lens of "protectors of the network" are going to really struggle with this transition. Experience demonstrates that district technology staff that have an industry IT background are sometimes security focused to a fault. On the other hand, those that emigrate to IT from the classroom may be more likely to see their roles as supportive and assistive—essentially seeing their roles as facilitators of the instructional use of technology. If a district is to successfully move to 1:1 and BYOD, a positive blend of these two perspectives is required.

With all of the additional users, security and network reliability will certainly be a challenge. And yes, even though they can sign agreements that say the opposite, there will still be users who want support on devices that the district knows nothing about. Issues of systemic risk management will be addressed more deeply in Chapter 4, but regardless of the type of risk, the only option is to just plan for 1:1, try it, figure it out, and make it work. This change is going to happen eventually, despite whatever the current opinions are. Can anyone imagine making the case that in 2050, kids will still be carrying around backpacks weighed down with fifty pounds of textbook materials? Nothing is so certainly written in the educational book of fate than the eventual advent of digital devices as the cornerstone of the learning environment. The sooner good solutions and processes are determined, the faster schools can get to a place where everyone benefits from 1:1 access.

This positive attitude will be needed when district personnel start considering the network capacity, security, and support issues that will certainly be high on the list of IT concerns in the transition to BYOD. On the capacity front, for those districts that were able to wire locations for future capacity during the heyday of infrastructure funding, capacity may not be a concern at all. Buildings with Category 5 or 6 fiber and high-capacity access points through all of their facilities and the switches to handle it may not need to do anything to handle the extra load presented by having every person in the building using the Internet at the same time. If a district is currently struggling with network capacity even in a scarcity model, the wiring upgrades will be necessary.

If that is the case, such an upgrade will need to precede moving to a 1:1 model. At least wiring and communications infrastructure are a one-time expenses and can be offset by nonstandard budget resources like E-rate funding. The E-rate program is administered by the Schools and Libraries Division of the Universal Service Administrative Company and has been subsidizing Internet and wireless infrastructure projects in the United States since 1997 (U.S. Department of Education, 2008). The worst-case scenario is that a major upgrade project or a total rewire is required. Such installations are considered capital expenses and could be bonded and financed over time, avoiding the huge one-time hit to a local budget that would typically prevent a project like this from being attempted. Infrastructure wiring is bonding acceptable as it retains its value over a long period of time with minimal depreciation. The same cannot be said for the computers that use the network itself. This is why bonding for infrastructure is a sound strategy but borrowing for devices that are worth half of what was paid six months later is not.

Other districts have the infrastructure network backbone needed but not the wireless-access capacity. With potentially hundreds of machines jumping on the network through wireless access at the same time, routers and access points designed to give everyone access to the school's wireless network need to be in place. Access testing with current networks is a good strategy here. A wireless access point that works fine with three students web browsing might not when a class of twenty-five all tries to hit a streaming video at the same time. Network and IT specialists can assist districts in planning for what is required for the expected populations in their location, and most vendors who work in this field have capacity surveys that they conduct as part of the upgrade process.

Security for Students and the Network

Once an appropriate network and wireless capacity is established, it is the IT director's job to worry about protecting it and students from those that would wish them ill. As mentioned, a balance between security and access is required. Of course, students and the network should be protected from predators, malicious viruses, phishing scams and the like. But if a network is so locked down that nobody can do anything productive on it, the purpose of having it is defeated. In his article "One Laptop, One Child," Wayne D'Orio (2008) writes that districts can't let "over-thinking" prevent technology support staff from seeing the potential benefits of this approach for all of the district's users. Among the possible solutions that are working across the country to enable this kind of access are preinstalled security access programs, separate virtual networks, and a new generation of wireless network management services.

REFLECTION/STUDY QUESTION

What is the state of your district's current network and wireless-access capacity? Do you have enough network strength to support a move to BYOD and handle every student's access to those resources? If not, what would you need to do to get there?

Security access protocols and hardware that provide wireless-network security have been developed and improved over the last decade. Cisco's Network Access Control (NAC) Appliance can be installed in a network configuration to provide a buffer between the primary network servers and the user. In the Connecticut State University system, all campuses are wireless, and everyone with a laptop is welcome to use the network. However, if someone wants to do this, she will need to have the companion Cisco software installed. This program communicates with the NAC Appliance to inspect a computer's configuration and ensure that it is protected from viruses and malware. After the application gives the machine a clean bill of health, it allows it on the network.

The Cisco NAC Appliance starts around $15,000, but there are other options as well. The Rainy River District in Ontario Canada uses InfoExpress's CyberGatekeeper with Dynamic Network Access Control (DNAC) to protect the school network. As more demand and competitors come to the market, prices for this type of service and the performance level of the solutions improve. The CyberGatekeeper folks say on their website that they can set up an NAC system in about an hour (InfoExpress, 2010). Regardless of the product, this prevention/protection approach is sensible and effective.

Another option is to set up a parallel virtual wireless network for student traffic only. What this accomplishes is the creation of a firewall between the servers that store mission-critical budget and student data and the instructional traffic that is dominated by students on the wireless side. D'Orio (2008) describes the setup in Forsyth County, Georgia, where the district uses a device that identifies established secure district computers and allows them on the network while all others are put on the district's virtual LAN. This allows the unfamiliar devices access to the Internet and pushes them through the district's Internet filters but at the same time keeps them away from the district's main data network. Of course, districts that have made the leap to store all of their data in the cloud can avoid the need for these parallel structures.

Growth in the wireless management market has facilitated the growth of a new generation of wireless management products to help districts manage this new challenge. In Brookfield, Connecticut, at Brookfield High School, IT staff depend on Meraki Systems to help manage the needed wireless access points they set up to enable a freshman 1:1 pilot program. Meraki provides an all-in-one management solution that allows district personnel set up multiple wireless access points for up to 10,000 users while providing real-time monitoring and alerts for security concerns. For those looking for a less expensive option that can be managed locally, companies like Open-Mesh provide similar management options at much lower entry price points.

The Jackson Local School district in Massillon, Ohio, has turned to Enterasys, one of a host of companies that have ramped up product offerings specifically to help schools manage the network-security aspect of their BYOD efforts. District's that do not have the internal IT technical capacity needed to secure filtered access for their wireless and wired networks, allow for asset tracking of appropriate devices, or create the desired user access levels will find vendors like Enterasys as helpful partners in dealing with these issues. ClassLink's LaunchPad is one of a series of new software programs that provide each user with a personalized desktop that is based in the cloud, is multiple platform and device neutral, and can even provide secure access to district network files. My friend Matt Mervis has created an entirely education- and student-centered application management ecosystem to help BYOD users stay organized and focused on the learning tasks at hand. By organizing applications through a central portal, the www.byodapps.com service reduces clutter, distraction, and risk, and improves productivity in 1:1 BYOD installations.

Unlike other destinations in the software world, where you really can get a free lunch, in network security and desktop management, there is definitely a "you get what you pay for" dynamic at work. User groups can help troubleshoot once you are underway, but if your internal IT staff lacks expertise in student and network security design, an external vendor's advice can be a good thing when creating your plans for BYOD access.

Planning for the Issues and Adjustments Needed for BYOD

In addition to the hardware and network side of the solution, there will also need to be new understandings generated among the user community if BYOD is going to work. While the issue of acceptable use policy will be explored in more detail in the next chapter, it is instructive to see how districts that are using BYOD are approaching security from the user's perspective. For example, the BYOD user agreement in Forsythe County, Georgia, requires students to agree that the only access points that they are officially allowed to use while in the school are the district's. This allows for filtering and security from the headend. We also know from experience that if a BYOD effort is simply announced rather than discussed and communicated well in advance, there will inevitably be some parent and constituent blowback regarding safety and security concerns. Misinformation and unknowns can lead to wild speculation and fear that will make your implementation more complicated.

For example, in a Connecticut district that moved aggressively to implement BYOD, there developed a perception among a parent group that the district was requiring them to buy devices and that there would be unfettered Internet access for all students. Neither of these things was true, and the misperceptions were eventually addressed, but it was clear that if we had done a better job preparing the community and engaging constituents in the run-up to the announcements, these self-inflicted barriers would have been less problematic. When it comes to student safety, parents are understandably concerned, and so dialogue in this area needs to be open and comprehensive. Effective preparation for BYOD must include information for parents about how students will be kept safe and taught good decision making, and even options for managing offsite Internet access with BYOD devices. Few issues are more emotional than the care of children, and BYOD implementations must keep this issue in the forefront of their planning processes.

Other management issues—like power supply, service, support, and maintenance of devices—are all important premigration topics. There are as many permutations to solutions here as there are districts using 1:1. For service and support for example, a key personnel concern is the time that will be needed to support all of these different devices. One approach is to state that the privilege of getting to bring your own device is that the owner takes responsibility for the device. This consideration would be part of a student's or a family's choice to use a personal device or to use one from the district pool. These provisions would all be part of a commonsense user agreement, like the one from Forsythe, which must be signed and turned in before a student can participate in BYOD, and helps form the lines of appropriate use. Finally, roles of existing IT staff may shift as well, as users become more self-efficient and the focus turns to network traffic. Regardless of the role, their contribution will be critical to your long-term success, and you should plan accordingly.

To summarize, Figure 2.3 represents the five major areas of prework required for successful implementation of BYOD and the critical issues to be addressed within each. We have reviewed the first four in this chapter, the fifth, regarding software and materials, is covered in detail in Chapter 3 but is included here so that you can see the entire range of preplanning BYOD issues.

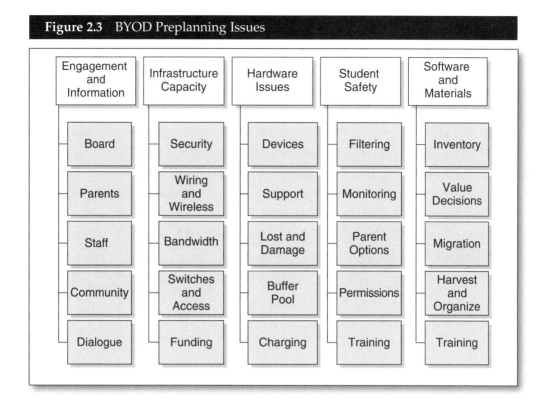

Figure 2.3 BYOD Preplanning Issues

Each of these items is explained in more detail on the *Digital Learning for All, Now* webpage **(http://www.digitallearningforall now.com)**. Clearly, the points raised here represent a superficial examination of the big issues that accompany the pursuit of a BYOD strategy. No chapter or article can possibly address all of the potential challenges that this process will entail, and any district that decides to wait until all of the answers are known will be waiting a long time. Technology develops rapidly, so new problems and new solutions are created and implemented on a daily basis. The key takeaway point here is that those who would argue against BYOD on purely technical grounds have not explored all of the potential options available to support the move.

More importantly is an understanding that a decision to move to BYOD is based on an intuitive sense that it represents the best chance to get schools where they need to be in the shortest amount of time. Put another way, the cumulative benefits outweigh the cumulative implementation problems. Once a district believes this to be true, history shows that people of good will and vision can work together to make it happen. Once this process is underway, the real work of a transition to 1:1 begins, and it has nothing to do with netbooks or networks. Technical barriers and technical changes can take place quickly.

The more substantive and critical changes regarding the development of a digital mindset is a more extended process, often taking years to accomplish. For 1:1 to achieve its promise, there must be a change in the culture, in the accompanying instructional systems, and in the focus of leadership itself. As many have said, when it comes to big ideas and change, it's the soft stuff that is the hard stuff.

With this in mind, Chapter 4 will explore the mindset barriers to change that are long established and supported by the print status quo. It is from this place that most of the excuses and barriers to 1:1 and BYOD come, so this chapter is designed help leaders anticipate and deal with them. Before we get there, though, we are going to examine the materials and resources side of the resource equation. Now that we have demonstrated how every district can access the hardware needed for a 1:1 transition, Chapter 3 will look at the software and instructional resource-acquisition strategies that will create savings over print and improve the quality of instruction in your district.

CHAPTER SUMMARY

In this chapter, we have explored the BYOD strategy in depth. First we reviewed the three trends that make BYOD possible: the pace of technology change, the maturation of the browser and open-source software, and a "customize or perish" market reality. Within this section, I introduced the 90/10 value equation as a way to determine the worth of commercial software as compared to open-source alternatives. From there, we looked at BYOD in industry and how the lessons learned there can improve ownership of learning in a school setting. We closed by looking at strategies that can be used to overcome the biggest barriers to success—namely, the perception that the district should pay, issues of equity, and security and policy challenges. The conclusion is that while not a perfect solution, BYOD is a viable strategy and most districts' best hope for getting to a 1:1 learning environment. We now turn our attention in Chapter 3 to how we can generate enough savings to pay for the devices and infrastructure that will be needed to support a BYOD implementation.

3

Take the Open Path

The Browser and Open Source—Saving Money and Improving Learning

Introduction to Open-Source Software

There Is Money to Be Saved

Even in districts where the BYOD participation rate is high, schools must plan for students who do not have their own devices for use in school. Regardless of the fiscal or personal reasons that lead to this decision, districts should to be ready for this eventuality. Purchasing the equipment needed to provide for these learners is an expense that you probably have not budgeted for, and this chapter details how districts can redirect resources to finance the purchase of these devices. This is accomplished by not paying for software for which schools can find legal and free alternatives and by reversing entrenched textbook-purchasing patterns. When applied systemically, districts that follow the strategies described in this chapter will be able to divert money to support improved information infrastructure purchases or anything else that the district needs.

First, let's address what qualifies as low-hanging budget fruit: simply saving money by eliminating unnecessary spending. If you have labored for hundreds of hours trimming every nonessential item from your spending plan and are certain there is nothing left to cut, this idea might seem fantastical. This is an understandable reaction, as the conditions that have made this cost-cutting strategy possible have only gained enough momentum to make it practical in the last few years.

If you are like most districts I have worked with, you annually allocate money in your technology budget for software and services that have become part of your assumed operational costs. Employees and students need software to do their work, and each computer and installed program carries with it a license fee to ensure legal use. That is no small matter, as appropriate application of copyright and intellectual property laws are nonnegotiable standards for all of us in public life. Regardless of the financial pressure, whatever acquisition strategy we pursue has to be legal and transparent. With the money annually spent on these licenses and the concurrent cost of trying to expand the percentage of users in your district, adhering to licensing standards makes continued use of these familiar programs an ongoing financial burden.

You will not have to look far to find the primary cost drivers. Do you use Microsoft Office (Word, PowerPoint, and Excel) for your back-office support applications? If you are locally hosting e-mail and calendar software, you may have an Outlook Exchange server. If you use PowerSchool for electronic grading, there are not only licenses but annual renewals too. Don't forget those operating system licenses. Since 1984, just about every computer purchased by a school has had either a Windows or Apple operating system installed on it. That OS may "come" with the computer, but that does not make it free.

Beyond these routine licenses that we buy for everyone, there are probably a few premium programs with specific operational functions that you have acquired in smaller but still significant numbers as well. Adobe PhotoShop for digital picture manipulation, Publisher or Illustrator for graphics production, perhaps even content-based media subscriptions for special lessons and units. All of these programs have become so ingrained in our daily habits that we take them for granted and accept that we must pay for them as part of the cost of doing our educational business.

The History of Open Source

This is not necessarily so anymore. There is another strategy for acquiring similar products, and it falls under the label FOSS: free and open-source software. For 90 percent of the work done in school, your purchased proprietary software has mature, stable, and completely legal open-source alternatives that you can use systemwide for free. From operating systems to back-office applications, e-mail, and even district data management programs, you do not have to spend another dime on software. In planning for next year's budget, why would you buy items that you know can be had elsewhere for nothing? Spending money unnecessarily is a status symbol for some, but if you are in an organization that fights for every operating dime and will have to do so for the foreseeable future, it's not prestige you are purchasing, it's waste. And this is not a one-time problem; it is a practice that keeps on burning dollars because it is repeated with each license purchase or renewal.

If open-source software sounds like a fairy tale from the "too good to be true" storybook, consider the long history of open-source software and the series of recent developments that have pushed the movement from a fringe labor of love to a viable alternative for all. From the earliest days of the personal computer revolution, there has always been a shared ethic among a small group of hardware and software enthusiasts that we are all in this together. These early collaborators believed that by working with each other and sharing their ideas, the quality of everybody's efforts would be improved.

A Browser Shows the Way

This community ethic and the programs they spawned had a constant presence in the development community but did not have a shared terminology and focus until early 1998. It was at this time when the owners of Netscape—spurred on by a paper promoting the value of letting the broader code-writing community's collaborative efforts inspire creative development of software products—announced they would make the code for their popular Communicator web browser public. The "open source" label for this process was created at a strategy session soon after, and the name has stuck ever since (Open Source Initiative, 2007). With the release of the code, and with an agreed-on tag to go with it, Netscape created an easily describable opportunity for anyone to create companion and utility software that enhanced the functionality of its product. While the actual long-term software impacts were slow to develop, the concept of leveraging the assets of a community beyond your own to add value to something of common purpose under the banner of open source was born.

Over time, the term *open source* has come to be applied not only to programs whose code is shared openly but also to any program that is made available to the public for free, whether the code is open or not. For example, OpenOffice, originally supported by Sun Microsystems, is both open code and license free. Its newer and web-based cousin Google Docs is also free, but its code is not public. Regardless of whether programs are code free or not, as long as they are license free, they present a real opportunity to save money for schools.

REFLECTION/STUDY QUESTION

Willingness to consider different strategies/pathways is a learned and culturally reinforced behavior. What is the comfort level of your current staff with the idea of trying something new? How many of your faculty or peers have tried open-source programs individually? Understanding the state of mind of your community as it relates to these issues will be critical when determining strategies for moving forward.

Open Source Comes of Age

While well known in the development community, through the mid-1990s, awareness of open-source programs among general users was still in a nascent phase. In the years following the coining of the term *open source*, this began to change. Open-source attention and opportunity built as the number of free programs that were available to the general public grew and their functionality improved. Hotmail, now ironically owned by Microsoft, was launched in the late 1990s with an explicit goal of being a free alternative to paid Internet service provider e-mail. This might seem odd today, but remember, this was the peak of the AOL era when most of us were paying $19.95 a month to have someone tell us we had mail and organize our Internet content. The currently ubiquitous browser emerged during this period as an important option for those able to surf the web without assistance and has always been in the "free to download" category. Starting with Netscape and Internet Explorer, and now extending to Netscape's offspring Firefox, Google's Chrome, and Apple's Safari, browsers remain the most universally applied example of functional programs you can download and use for free.

The first decade of the 21st century saw open source expand its reach as more complex functional programs were developed under this same banner. OpenOffice, probably the best known in a new wave of free consumer-level programs that went beyond browsing and e-mail, enjoyed a significant level of user support. In its first three years of release, OpenOffice was downloaded over 20 million times (OpenOffice.org, 2011). While OpenOffice and similar options have had loyal followers, through 2008, they did not have enough market share to make them a true threat to the licensed program establishment. Programs like Microsoft Office still dominated the scene and usually found their way onto just about every PC in a business and school setting. In the last few years, however, three additional phenomena have joined together to accelerate the open-source dynamic and forever alter our ideas of what software is and how we should expect it to work.

The Big Move to Make Software Small: Impact of the App

In July 2008, Apple used its iTunes music software to launch what it called the *App Store*. What has happened since is important to our story just as much for what it says about culture and what we perceive as about actual program functionality. This is still significant because when it comes to human beings and our behavior, culture and perception matter. It is easy to forget, but the now taken for granted "app" has only been around in its present form for about four years. Begun by Apple, but now joined in the fray by Android and Blackberry, the app ecosystem has completely changed our collective impression of what software is, how it works, and what we should expect it to cost.

Think back to the "old days" of software. In 1996, when I first went into business for myself, I paid $495 for my first personal copy of Microsoft Office. At that time, the release of "Office '97 Premium" came on one CD, and that license allowed me to use those precious programs on one PC. I upgraded those programs several times over the years, and I remember vividly my shock and sense of awe the first time it took two CDs to install it. Remember when you would put that magic CD in and the installation utility would tell you how much hard-drive space you would need, and how long it would take, to transfer all of the required information to your PC? I also recall my growing frustration that with every new release in 2000, 2003, 2007—because of all the "amazing new features"—that required hard-drive space number got bigger, and more processing power was needed to run the new version just at the old speed.

And such it was for software. Big footprints, restrictive licenses, ensured obsolescence for both programs and hardware, and an endless treadmill of upgrades and expenses. No wonder schools fell so far behind their business-based peers in the technology race: It cost a fortune to just keep up. The software world has now been turned upside down. Today, on my iPhone, I have an app called *Documents-To-Go* that will run all of the programs from that 1996 Office suite, and it cost me just $9.99, and that is expensive by app standards. As mentioned in Chapter 2, the average cost of the literally hundreds of thousands of apps that are available is less than $2 (Zibreg, 2011).

The impact of these easy-to-use and inexpensive apps is that in just a few years, our primary idea of what software is has been transformed from an inflexible, costly, all-or-nothing proposition into a customized, feature-specific, almost disposable and entirely affordable marketplace. I routinely carry between 75 and 100 apps on my iPad and iPhone, the combined cost of which is less than $150. At least half of all my apps are free. This environment has sharpened the consumer edge and turned them skeptical regarding traditional software pricing and packaging. We want it cheap and easy, and the open-source community is willing to oblige.

The Rise of Google

Reinforcement for the growing demand for affordable software can be found in the concurrent success of Gmail, GoogleDocs, and the increasing cultural influence of Google. Starting in 2004, as a way to build on its search engine success, Google began offering a simple to use and free e-mail system. Beginning on a brilliant "by invitation only" marketing basis, Gmail quickly garnered the elusive "cool" distinction, and its explosive growth as a destination beyond the search window began. Google will not officially say how many users it has, but in just eight years of existence, most estimates put it at well over 200 million. Hotmail still has more users, but this is not about the number of accounts as much as it is about what Google is giving people who use their service for free.

Early on, it became clear that Google's exceptional e-mail client was just the beginning, and the real long-term value of Gmail was as an entryway to a suite of ever-expanding and incredibly effective tools that would also be free to users. Relentlessly they were added— Google Maps, shared calendars, contact managers, Picasa for photos, Blogster for blogs, and then, in late 2006, the launch of what would become Google Docs. When this web-based spreadsheet, presentation, and word-processing package joined the already formidable and constantly updated group of free Google tools, users started to take notice of what was underway.

Combined with what was happening in the app universe, Google-driven behavior really helped solidify consumer belief in two new realities. First, *free* does not have to mean cheap or nonfunctional. There are features in free Google Docs and in free apps, like real-time collaborative work abilities, that are better than anything out there available at any price. Second was the idea that acquiring software did not necessarily mean a trip down to Staples to spend a fortune on a stack of CDs. Software could now be easily acquired through downloads and was much leaner, more feature specific, and less expensive than we had come to expect from their boxed and installed predecessors. Additionally, and even more significantly, in the case of Google Docs, you did not even have to download the program to enjoy its functionality. You access it through the browser. Welcome to the cloud.

REFLECTION/STUDY QUESTION

What is the percentage of your staff that has a phone or tablet that uses apps? How many have a Gmail account? Knowing these numbers will give you a sense of how open they may be to trying something different when it comes to proprietary software. How can you build on these experiences when thinking of how to introduce them to institutional applications that can save money across the district?

The Answer Is in the Cloud

As introduced in the last chapter, the emergence of web-based, Web 2.0, or "cloud-based" applications and data storage have not only reduced the requirements of hardware but have simplified software acquisition as well. Applications that can be designed to run remotely through the web, or through the cloud, do not have to be downloaded at all. Subsequently, they work equally well from any location using any piece of hardware that will run a browser. The bar has been lowered, and the options available to consumers have exploded: small, low footprint, web-based and free tools that can all get the job done. How else to explain the emergence of Quixey?

Quixey.com is an application search engine. There are now so many ways to do whatever it is you want to do that there is a search engine to help you sort through them all. So, if you want to do keep track of out-of-classroom expenses on instructional materials, for example, type that into Quixey, and it will return all of the available results for Apple, Blackberry, Android, Windows, web, and so on. As an indicator of open source's impact and availability, when in Quixey, you can sort out the search results, just as you can in the Apple App Store, by whether the found software options are free or paid. And that is part of the point here: Regardless of the software job to be done, there is almost always a way to do it for free. E-mail, documents, publishing—you can do them all free, free, free. As a school, or maybe just as someone who would rather get something for nothing, that should get your attention.

How Much Can We Save?

The wealth of free options in the software market has had the collateral market benefit of lowering the general price of software for everyone. In the educational market especially, licenses for office suites that used to cost hundreds can now be had for less than $60 per seat. With so many free options, lowering prices is the only way for vendors selling licenses to stay in the game. This trend is also being fueled by the price-depressing dynamic of the current battle for market share between Google and Microsoft. In a tussle of titans to win consumers with low prices, when one starts by declaring "free" as the opening bid, all we can do is sit back and enjoy the show.

Whatever your school's or district's software choices are, the goal should be to pay as little as possible and to use those precious recovered funds to support other areas of your educational program. We are in a unique procurement time, and the opportunity to lock in long-term institutional software savings may never be better. Act now or forever regret signing those annual renewal purchase orders. And just in case you are thinking that the savings may not be worth the change, I have provided an analysis tool for you to add up how much you are currently spending on licenses that could be eliminated. Most find the total surprising, as the costs for software are added slowly over many budget years. Add a license every year or two and incrementally, it takes up more and more of your resources. Take a few minutes to fill in Figure 3.1. An electronic version is available for download on the *Digital Learning for All, Now* webpage (click on the "Digital Resources" button).

Figure 3.1   What Are You Spending? Part 1 (Productivity Software)

Area	License Type	X Users	Annual Expense
Office products			
E-mail			
Webpages			
Student info/data			
Specialty software			
Total Annual Productivity Software Expense:			

Open-Source Productivity Software Resources

To demonstrate just how target rich this environment is, I have provided just a few examples of available productivity programs that could replace your current paid desktop and office software in Figures 3.2–3.4 (beginning on page 62). These tables are available electronically on the *Digital Learning for All, Now* webpage with active links to appropriate software. Resources for instructional materials follow in the next section of this chapter. This is not an exhaustive list, and there are new options available and released by the day. For example, I just did a search for "free personal e-mail" that returned over 1,400 possibilities. The options provided in the following grids are simply examples and suggested starting points for a discussion on the potential for open source in your school community. All of listings are solidly in the mainstream, with millions of downloads or users with experience in each. If you know of other great options that

I have missed or if a link no longer works, leave me a message on the *Digital Learning for All, Now* blog or send me an e-mail through the webpage: info@digitallearningforallnow.com.

Figure 3.2   Open-Source Operating Systems

Program	Location	Notes/Guidance
Ubuntu	http://www.ubuntu.com/	A mature and stable open-source operating system based on Linux code, Ubuntu has millions of users and thousands of built-in applications, and is an outstanding option for free operating system users.
Opensolaris	http://hub.opensolaris.org/bin/view/Main/	A viable option from Oracle, Opensolaris was originally developed by Sun Microsystems. While not as widely used by mainstream users as Ubuntu, Opensolaris does have an active user community.

Figure 3.3   Open-Source Back-Office Suites

Program	Location	Notes/Guidance
OpenOffice	www.openoffice.org	Flexible (Win, Mac, Linux) and compatible with all major office suites (i.e., Microsoft Office). Includes Writer (word processing), Impress (presentation), Calc (spreadsheet), Draw (illustrations), and Base (database). OpenOffice is available as a download.
Google Docs	www.google.com	Flexible (web based) and compatible with all major office suites (i.e., Microsoft Office). Includes word processor, spreadsheet, presentation, and illustration programs. Integrates well with all of the other available Google tools. Google Docs runs online.
IBM Lotus Symphony	http://www.03.ibm.com/software/lotus/symphony	Based on the OpenOffice code, this is a direct competitor to Microsoft Office. Contains Documents, Spreadsheets, and Presentations. Symphony is available as a download.
ThinkFree	http://member.thinkfree.com	Flexible (web based), multi-device, and platform, ThinkFree attempts to mirror Microsoft-type menus and feel. Contains word-processor, spreadsheet, and presentation applications.

Figure 3.4   Open-Source Productivity, Learning, and Communication Suites

Program	Location	Notes/Guidance
Gmail	www.google.com	Google is the beast in this market: excellent e-mail security and spam protection, calendars, tasks, video and chat capability—all built in and all free. Strong administrative management tools through Postini available at some cost.
Microsoft Live@edu	http://www .microsoft.com/ education/en-us/ solutions	Microsoft's cloud-based answer to Google—an Outlook-like experience available through the web and mobile devices. Includes calendars and document sharing.
Thunderbird	http://www .mozilla.org/ en-US/ thunderbird/	A free e-mail client from one of the founding branches of the open-source family tree, Thunderbird is the offspring of Netscape Communicator and is from the folks at Mozilla (maker of the current Firefox browser).
Blogger	http://www blogger.com	Owned by Google since 2003, Blogger allows users to create and publish their own blogs for free. As many as a billion blogs have been created using this service.
Moodle	http://moodle .org/	An open-source learning platform, Moodle is a feature-rich and easy-to-use program that can host lessons, units, or courses. Moodle is the software we use to host all of EDUCATION CONNECTION's Center for 21st Century Skills courses.
WordPress	http://wordpress .com/	An open source program for text/document integration developed by Matt Mullenweg, Wordpress has been downloaded millions of times and is highly flexible and adaptable for integration with other open source programs.
Wikispaces	http://www .wikispaces .com/	Easy to use and quite flexible, wikis are web based posting and sharing boards that allow communities to easily create electronic exchange areas to for the good of everyone in the group.
Tumblr	http://www .tumblr.com/	A highly functional, multiple platform web 2.0 blogging tool, tumblr allows for easy cross device program integration (post e-mails and tweets to your blog, etc.) of text, pictures and just about anything else.

For live links to this software, go to **http://www.digitallearningforallnow.com** and click on the "Digital Resources" button, select the appropriate chapter from the drop-down menu, and enter the password **D L F A N** (all uppercase).

If you have not already done so, I would encourage you and your peers to install and test run these programs to see what they are like. In areas in which the open-source option is the dominant market force already, as with web browsers and blogs, for example, there will be no performance gap between the paid and free program. With no actual or perceived difference in performance, implementation is easy. When it comes to the big office programs where most educators have spent the majority of their computer time over the last twenty years, this perception may be different. Many have been using Microsoft Word and PowerPoint for so long, it is hard for any program, no matter how effective, to come out ahead in a direct comparison between the free and the paid option. Just as it is with any change in an area that is familiar, there will be resistance in your community to giving up these long-used software programs.

Strategies for Supporting Open-Source Change

To prepare for this inevitability and to increase your chances of success, before even suggesting any open-source program as an alternative, I would suggest that you read Chapter 6 of this book. Any change that impacts the entire system will have profound implications for human behavior, and Chapter 6 is devoted to understanding the change process and modeling the skills of positive forward movement. Change is always messy and unpredictable; Chapter 6 will provide you with tools you can use to increase your chances of success. Having said that, be assured that each of the following four strategies will integrate with, and be supported by, the lessons learned in that chapter.

Strategy 1: Focus on Value

To start, I would refer you back to the 90/10 value equation that we introduced as a way to evaluate hardware in Chapter 2. The point of 90/10 is to focus on value and not absolute performance. In other words, it's not about what is the best software; it's about what is the best functional value in the software marketplace for the money. It would be nice if schools could afford to buy the best of everything, but they can't. The economics of public education is tight, and there is no relief in sight. Don't ask whether the free program has better features than the available proprietary one; ask whether the open source program is a better value than the proprietary option, and what could be done with the money saved in making the change.

If we did a feature-by-feature comparison of the Google Docs word-processing program and Microsoft Word and listed them side by side, I am confident that there are tools in Word that are not available in Google Docs. One concern I hear about all the time is how much easier it is to format text in Microsoft Word. I agree—in fact, the publisher of this book, Corwin, requires authors to submit their manuscripts in Microsoft Word for this reason. This fact is not in dispute, and for those rare assignments where formatting is truly critical, maybe every school should have a handful of Word-licensed machines available for students or staff to use for this purpose. My questions are, what percentage of assignments fall into that category, and is purchasing a $60 license for every student just in case they might have to do an assignment with perfect margins a smart use of the district's money?

In applying the 90/10 value equation, it has been my experience that very few proprietary programs survive this analysis. There are exceptions, and they usually fall in the areas of network security, student data management, or specialty instructional software. Even in these areas, there are now new open-source options, such as Opensis for student data, that have been to be proven stable, secure, and effective. Each district must ask and answer its own 90/10 value analysis question, and I expect that there will be some variation in the answers from district to district. One thing is certain, however: If you do not go through the exercise, you will end up paying for software and features that, on a value basis, you cannot possibly afford or justify.

Strategy 2: Balance the Pitch Between Function and Savings

The second strategy to assist in a software transition is to be sure that when you go to sell or promote a move to an open-source program, you balance your software pitch between functionality and savings. Using the 90/10 value equation is a great way to make a strategic procurement decision, but some will take that as a sign that money matters more than quality. If the perception builds that you are willing to make everyone's life more difficult just to save a few bucks, it will drain from the political capital you will need for more important educational changes later in the process. It is important to be honest with users by discussing both the advantages and disadvantages of whatever new software program you are moving to regardless of the reasons you made the move.

In my agency, when we switched from Microsoft Exchange to Google for e-mail, calendars, contacts, and tasks, we were up-front about feature loss. At the time we switched, for example, there was no way to mark an outgoing message in Google as having "high importance." Leaving aside the reality that some people marked every message that way, in our trainings, we talked about work-arounds for that shortcoming, and how this was the kind of thing that Google, if they heard enough about it from users, might eventually change it. We then quickly moved on to emphasize features that our new Gmail system would have that Outlook did not. We emphasized the collaborative features, the fact that access is consistent no matter what workstation or mobile device you are using, the flexibility of customization, and the overall ease of use. From the beginning, we presented Google as a better alternative that just happened to cost less.

REFLECTION/STUDY QUESTION

Who on your staff is already using one or more of the open-source programs listed in this chapter? Having them come forward to advocate and share their experiences with open source can provide powerful examples for others and help reduce the fear of the unknown and underscore the power of the 90/10 value equation.

Strategy 3: Support the Change, Support Each Other, Support Yourself

The third strategy for easing the change into a systemwide open-source alternative is creating support networks and training sessions as a way ease people's fears in advance of the switch. One of the most commonly stated phobias associated with open source is the loss of the single point of support contact. Many of us cling to a memory of the time when there was a live software support infrastructure. Remember the 800 number that came with your installation CD? There was a promise of a live customer-service professional on call for us 24/7. This was one of the privileges of purchasing a software license, and it always served as a comforting safety net if there were problems. Mention open source and the first objection you may hear is, "Who do I call if I have a complaint about a free software program?"

Here are three things to keep in mind when you hear this objection. First of all, ask folks if they have actually tried to call a live person at Microsoft or Adobe for software support recently. Live, free support is a thing of the past. If you devoted the same energy required to find an actual support number and then navigate through the menu maze to just using the web to solve the problem for yourself, you would be done in half the time. Second, open-source programs are built and supported by the greater public community. For each of the major open-source programs, there are literally hundreds of web-pages devoted to sharing support throughout that program's user community. Answers are just as easy to find as they are on the com-mercial side, and users genuinely want to share what they know with others. Mainstream open-source programs are no longer the buggy and error prone programs that they used to be. Anyone who tried early versions of OpenOffice experienced a crash or two as he was getting started. Users will find today's programs stable and feature rich. I will repeat: "Going open" does not equate to going cheap or giving up quality.

Additionally, it is important to note that in a transition to open source, solving a problem or making the effort to learn a new way to do something is not the end of the world; it is a required 21st century skill. I understand this will be of little solace when you are the one with the problem, but it is a critical consideration when taking the long view of this process. One of the key points to be made in Chapter 6 is that to be effective 21st century educators, we need to be able to demonstrate for our students the very skills we believe they will need to be successful. Familiarity with existing software is a matter of com-fort and predictability.

These are influential factors for people, and you minimize them at your own risk. Nonetheless, we cannot expect students to be flexible, solve problems, and overcome the small issues that come up when trying something new if we cannot do these same things ourselves. At the EDUCATION CONNECTION, before we ever asked our staff to make the transition from Outlook to Google, our entire central office staff as well as a pilot group had made the change and lived with the new software ourselves. This allowed us to speak about the conversion process and support issues firsthand, and to demonstrate our own willingness to change before we asked others to do the same.

Strategy 4: Get Out of Your Building

The fourth strategy to support this change is to do a little research and find a school or district in your region that has made a similar transition and go and visit them. What you and your peers will find is that everyone in the target school is still alive and well and the busi-ness of schooling continues. Go ask questions, watch them use it, and get a sense that all will be well. Actually seeing others using software in a new and productive way is a powerful modeling activity that helps break down that fear of the unknown. There will be more about managing the change process in Chapter Six, but here is a summary of the first four transition strategies that we have examined so far:

Figure 3.5   Supporting Strategies for a Transition to Open-Source Productivity Software

Software Change Support Strategy Review	
1. Focus on value	Use the 90/10 value equation in presentations and discussions. It is not about finding the best program; it is about finding the best value.
2. Balance function and savings	Open-source programs often have unique features of their own—balance your "sales pitch" between the utility of the function and the money that the district will save.
3. Support the staff	Provide training and support and be proactive about showing your peers how to find answers on their own. Support the program, support each other, and be able to support yourself.
4. Go see a model	Find a school or district that has made a transition to open-source software and go see them in action. This will help to break down the fear of the unknown.

Stop Digging!

One final point before we move on to open-source instructional materials: if you advocate for this long enough, you will eventually hear someone object to a move to open source by saying, "But we have so much invested in our current platform, it would be a waste to leave it now." This is compounded by the fact that many software companies, aware of these trends, have started to bundle and wrap licenses, so switching means leaving many programs at the same time rather than the much easier to manage one at a time that we would probably prefer. Either way, my translation of this objection comes down to "we have dug this hole so deep our only option is to just keep on digging." As I mentioned earlier in this chapter, I know the financial pain of being on the upgrade train. New versions of Office every three years, a new version of Quicken every year, operating systems upgrades, and a nice fee to go right along with them each time. I know schools have invested significant money on software in the past, and that makes it hard to let go. But seriously, we are at the end of the line; the truth is, we can't afford it anymore. Happily, we are in a time when this fiscal reality does not have to mean a diminished level of organizational performance. The past will not be prologue here; it is time to move on to a better value position.

This is a realization that millions of educator users across the globe have come to, with more joining the movement every day. Using Google Docs as an example, a quick check on their global use map at the time of publication found users on every continent but Antarctica and in schools using forty different languages worldwide (Google, 2011). So enticing is the promise of open source, instances of adoption are going beyond education and into the municipal and business communities as well. Indiana's Department of Education INACCESS program uses and promotes open-source solutions for schools statewide. In an effort to save money and boost productivity, thousands of enterprises/businesses have migrated to open-source platforms and programs. From huge global institutions with tens of thousands of users to small public school districts like Newtown here in my home state of Connecticut, examples of successful transition are easy to find. If they can do it, you can to.

Open Source and Online Instructional Materials

A Target-Rich Environment

In my exploration of the productivity side of open source, I made the case based on value. I felt this emphasis was needed to help overcome the perception that free software might not be as effective as paid. No such effort is needed for the acquisition of educational resources. When it comes to instructional materials online, there is a variety of options available that are free and of exceptional quality. With thoughtful effort, highly effective, low- or no-cost digital resources are available to support any instructional program, including a migration to the Common Core State Standards. All of the same spirit and intent notions related to productivity open-source software apply instructionally, but there are two additional factors that make an even more powerful case for classroom use. First is the inherent advantage of using anything digital over paper to prepare students for a digital life, and second is the growing influence and maturation of the "wiki culture."

The Text Is Dead: Long Live the Text

As explored in Truth 2, to build 21st century skills, students need ready use of the necessary digital tools. This extends beyond hardware to the instructional materials used in their studies. If 21st century preparation is the accepted mission of public schools, then we must agree that the text is dead and say, "Long live the text." In other words, digital beats print as a platform for preparing students for life in a digital age. With this in mind, we need to go one step further to make sure we get digital right. It is not just the format of the material that is a concern when making the transition to a 21st century learning environment; it is the very structure of it and how it is used as well. As we will explore in Chapter 5, realigning goals for learning with 21st century expectations requires more than just a superficial shift in instructional materials.

One of the basic limitations of the textbook format as a teaching tool is its frozen-in-time, one-size-fits-all, linear presentation of static content materials. The barrier of the book in a digital-age learning environment is not the words on the page; it is the expectation that this one book could possibly be the best available resource for each student in any given classroom. When we give a student one book, we present them with a single form of the information. Here is what you need to know, now learn it—as if in any part of modern life, there is just one place or one way to find anything.

REFLECTION/STUDY QUESTION

Have you ever heard your peers say that your school has to continue to use texts because that is what students will be using when they get to college? You might ask, what college? More and more university programs are transitioning to digital resources. Discuss how teaching and learning will shift with a move toward digital and what the implications are for goals, strategies, and assessments.

As many authors before me have emphatically stated, in an information age, student success beyond school will not be obtained through passive receipt of information. Knowledge workers need to be skilled enough to go out and get what they need, process it, evaluate it, and construct their own new learning from all the sources they have gathered. When even technically skilled students who do not have these information-seeking and information-evaluation skills are dropped into real-world settings, the results are predictably disappointing. Alan November's chapter "Technology Rich, Information Poor" in James Bellanca and Ronald Brandt's *21st Century Skills: Rethinking How Students Learn* (2010) makes this point beautifully.

Retrofitting Is a Waste

Educators want to do what is best for kids, but for many, the first pathway they choose for modernizing learning materials is to simply purchase an electronic textbook. This involves the vendor taking the print version, digitizing it, and transferring it to a flash drive, CD, or the web. And publishers are happy to oblige this instinct, as for them, it is the shortest and most profitable distance between two points. It is interesting that many charge the exact same money, or even more, for the digital version of their print texts. What? Putting that aside, this is more than just making a print source digital; it is about the nature of the text as well. Sure, a digital version increases some flexibility of use, but the same limitations of source, complexity, and perspective remain.

Turning print textbooks into digital ones is a classic technology-enabled retrofit that is hard to justify. It is no different from spending $2,000 on a laptop and projector so a teacher can convert overhead transparencies into PowerPoint slides. More colorful and fancy, for sure, and the adult learns some new skills, but on a pedagogical level, there is minimal improvement in learning for the expense involved. This waste is compounded when you consider the potential tools and strategies for increased student engagement that could be funded with that same cash.

Put simply, avoid the retrofit. If you are going to go through the effort of upgrading your instructional resources, why not really improve them so that they are actually aligned with the world in which students will be living and working? When you reengineer or rethink the use of the textbook, you start with the question, what is the best and most cost-efficient way to replicate an appropriate instructional environment for students? When you look at today's available resources, the answer to that question cannot possibly be a single textbook in any form.

Before we explore more appropriate electronic instructional options, take a few moments and tally the annual cost of supporting teaching and learning in a print environment. The digital version of Figure 3.6 (see page 72) is on the *Digital Learning for All, Now* webpage and will allow you to easily demonstrate what resources would be made available for redeployment in a BYOD effort. Remember, this is more than just textbook expenses; there are other costs related to supporting a print-based school environment that can also be reduced or eliminated in a completely digital system.

Figure 3.6   What Are You Spending? Part 2 (Print Materials)

Area	K–5	6–8	9–12	Annual Expense
Copier contracts				
Copy paper and supplies				
Printers and supplies				
Postage				
General texts (for all)				
Course texts (for a class)				
Periodicals/newspapers				
All other print subscriptions				
Other				
Total Annual Print Era Outlay:				
Total Cost / # of students = Current Annual Per-Pupil Cost of Print				

To download an electronic version of this table so you can adapt it and use it in your own school community, go to **http://www.digitallearningforallnow.com,** click on the "Digital Resources" button, select the appropriate chapter from the drop-down menu, and enter the password **D L F A N** (all uppercase).

Free, Engaging, and Rigorous

I'll bet you were not expecting the number in that spreadsheet to be that high. If you have seen the costs associated with high-end video or resource subscriptions on the web, you may be thinking that it will be difficult to replace these print resources with less expensive digital ones. Not necessarily. In the summer of 2011, I ran a U.S. history text-book–replacement workshop for teachers in the EDUCATION CONNECTION service area. The idea was to meet as a group of volunteers and to work together to harvest enough resources to replace our U.S. history texts in a week's worth of time. My colleague Kali Rohr and I set up a Moodle course outline based on the ten chronological eras associated with the national U.S. History Content Standards. Within these segments, we created placeholders for the types of resources we were looking for to organize the diversity of sources: descriptive texts, historical first-person narratives, primary source documents, and preexisting units and lessons. Using just standard search engines to scour the Internet, six volunteer teachers in less than a week gathered and indexed over 150 resources and lessons in chronological order. Any classroom with 1:1 access in any of these districts is now free to choose an open-source alternative to their stock U.S. history textbook.

Beyond the potential savings to the five participating districts, the best thing about this project is the variety of resources now available to teachers. They have access to multiple pathways of addressing the same topics from different authors' perspectives and in several formats. Teachers can now create research and exploration tasks with multiple complex texts, all within the same digital course. By having students work with multiple resources in a variety of tasks and formats, our teachers can begin to replicate the kind of work that students will encounter in modern work settings. Doing this work well involves foundational skill fluencies that have been identified and supported by all who have written on this topic in the last decade. As Bernie Trilling and Charles Fadel (2009) state plainly, "In the 21st century, everyone's level of information literacy and fluency will need to rise" (p. 65).

As I mentioned, we were able to accomplish our U.S. history collection task at minimal expense; volunteer teachers harvesting open-source and royalty-free teaching resources equals a textbook-replacement project that was free to anyone that helped create it. There were some minor costs—my agency donated the rooms where we met, and I used some grant resources to pay for technical assistance on the Moodle server—but overall, the reality is that we created an instructional resource that is more aligned with student interests and learning needs and costs less—a lot less—than the textbook it replaces. Even if participating districts had paid their teachers to participate in this or similar projects, the value of the results as replacements for texts would far outweigh the cost of the labor.

As an additional benefit, this is the type of work that is also encouraged through the new Common Core State Standards. We will explore the specific alignment between the new standards and consensus 21st century skills in Chapter 5, but there is significant overlap, especially as it relates to higher-order thinking. In the recently released Common Core Publishers Criteria, which are designed to provide guidance to those building curricula based on the new standards, the standards authors state, "To become career and college ready, students must grapple with a range of works that span many genres, cultures, and eras and model the kinds of thinking and writing students should aspire to in their own work" (Coleman & Pimentel, 2011, p. 5). Single texts simply do not contain this kind of work and source variety. Even if a district wanted to provide the multiple complex print sources called for in the standards, to do so in each content area would cost a fortune. With digital resources, schools can mirror real-world work using real-world resources and can meet the spirit of the new standards.

Finally, digital content allows for preparation in an area mostly ignored by the Common Core: all other nonprint forms of information. While clearly an advancement in some ways, there is a significant blind spot in the new text-heavy standards for the role that audio and visual representations play in 21st century communications and content knowledge. These are legitimate goals for learning, and to not give students practice in an area that will clearly be important to their future is a Common Core problem that is easily rectified.

Wiki Is Not a Four-Letter Word

Inexpensive and high quality—welcome to the digital world of open-source instructional resources. It does seem counter to what we have come to expect. Clichés about getting what you pay for and no free lunch come to mind. What makes this effort possible is a unique manifestation of the same open-source ethic described earlier in this chapter but applied to sharing the sharing of general expertise and knowledge. The wiki phenomenon is essentially the crowdsourcing of knowledge, and it is a tradition that runs strong and deep in the educational community.

It is somewhat ironic that for many educators, hearing the word *wiki* usually generates a reaction of scorn worthy of older four-letter words. Early in the Wikipedia era, the idea of a wiki was associated with sloppy scholarship and bad information. Still today, despite many studies that have compared the overall accuracy of its content favorably to other more traditional sources, the mention of Wikipedia in a high school faculty meeting will invariably generate gasps of derision and academic horror. The essential question is, can everyone be collectively smarter than anyone? Teachers with an open mind who answer yes have a world of opportunity because it seems that just about every teacher who owns a keyboard and a mouse is willing to share.

REFLECTION/STUDY QUESTION

Do you use or allow the use of wikis in your classroom or school? In what contexts or settings does the use of a crowdsourced knowledge base make sense? Consider as a community how to recognize the value of crowdsourcing while putting the wiki into the proper context.

We can all be grateful that teachers are a giving lot. They care about their students and are willing to share generously with other teachers to help them support the education of their students as well. The end result is a digital world so full of educational resources and materials that the central problem is never that there is nothing to be found on a topic, but rather that there is so much to be found that it can be difficult to sort through it all. And certainly, as in any area of the World Wide Web, there is sorting to be done. At a minimum, teachers will need to classify finds according to grade level, subject alignment, appropriate sourcing, complexity, and overall quality. Having a clear outcome in mind and using similar criteria as you evaluate results are critical for selecting what resources fit your curriculum best.

There can be a teaching opportunity in this acquisition process as well. As we will discuss in Chapter 6, it is important that educators be able to demonstrate and model the skills they expect from their students. As you or your faculty develop digital resource lists for use in your courses, make finding additional resources in a variety of formats that support key goals part of student assignments. Teach them to employ the same evaluative criteria, and see what they find. The professional educator should be the final arbiter, but just in the process, students will be exercising one of their most important 21st-century skills and helping the school build its instructional resource base at the same time.

Open Sharing of Resources

It has always been the goal of the open-source movement to share everyone's knowledge with the understanding that when we all participate, we all benefit. The creation and sharing of open-source teaching resources has a broad base because while there are few teachers who know how to write the software code needed to produce new open-source programs, every educator has an instructional expertise that they can share. Just as eBay facilitated the worldwide connection of communities of people who have shared purchasing interests, wikis, blogs, and webpages have brought together educators with similar intellectual or cultural passions. The result is a happy combination of improved quality, greater diversity, better mission alignment, and reduced cost.

I have provided, on the following pages, three different categories of instructional resources that can be used free of charge to improve any instructional program (see Figures 3.7–3.9). The first are straight digital textbook alternatives, the second are compilation sites to support specific content areas, and the third are general open-source support user communities. All of these and more are available, like the productivity programs from earlier in this chapter, with direct digital access through my Corwin *Digital Learning for All, Now* webpage. If you know of other resources that I have missed that you believe your peers should know about, leave me a message on the *Digital Learning for All, Now* blog page or send me an e-mail.

Figure 3.7   Digital Textbook Alternatives

Resource	Location	Notes/Guidance
CK–12 Foundation	http://www .ck12.org/ flexbook/	CK–12 Foundation is a nonprofit with a mission to reduce the cost of textbook materials for the K–12 market. Using an open-content, web-based collaborative model termed the *FlexBook*, these resources could be used as a foundational or supplemental text.
Khan Academy	http://www .khanacademy .org	The Khan Academy is a content video resource library. At the vanguard of the "Flipping the Classroom" movement, teachers can supplement the content delivery usually accomplished through textbooks with these resources.
MoodleShare	http://www .moodleshare. org	As they state on their site, "MoodleShare is a community of Moodlers sharing their Moodles, Moodle Sites, and Moodle Lessons."
California Open Source Textbook Project	http://www .opensourcetext .org/	One of the organizational hubs of California's effort to create a totally digital alternative to print texts, the COSTP site has a variety of good links and information.

Wikibooks	http://en.wikibooks.org/wiki/Main_Page	Lots of free and open digital resources in several content areas and reading levels.
Gutenberg Project	http://www.gutenberg.org/	Founded by the late Michael Hart, Project Gutenberg offers over 36,000 free ebooks to download to your PC, Kindle, Android, iOS, or other portable device.
COSTP World History Project	http://en.wikibooks.org/wiki/COSTP_World_History_Project	The prototype for the first shift to digital resources, this wikibook can serve as an alternative world history resource.
The People's Physics Book	http://www.siprep.org/science/physics/PPB.cfm	A product of California's shift to digital resources, this physics resource is among the best examples of how high-quality digital resources can emerge. This version is hosted by Saint Ignatius Prep in San Francisco.

Figure 3.8   Compilation Sites of Content- or Task-Specific Resources

Resource/Program	Location	Notes/Guidance
Center for 21st Skills Resource List	http://ctcareerchoices.org/index.php/about/tools	A list of free or open-source programs that the EDUCATION CONNECTION's Center for 21st Century Skills uses to support its courses.
Saugus Union Software Resources	http://community.saugususd.org/jklein/files/135/587/OSS.pdf	A software list from Jim Klein, director of Information Services and Technology for Saugus Union school district in California. Eight pages long, this resource list has everything from back office to programming and everything in between.
Open Source Program List	http://www.doe.in.gov/olt/docs/opensource_programs.pdf	Compiled by Dr. David Thornburg, a tireless and effective advocate for open-source education, this list is hosted on the Indiana Department of Education webpage.
Educational Freeware	http://www.educational-freeware.com/	In return for viewing a few sidebar sponsors' ads, you will have access to hundreds of links and programs with free web-based or downloadable free educational resources.
Gizmo's Freeware	http://www.techsupportalert.com/view/educational	Staffed by volunteers, Gizmo's keeps a running list of educational freeware that are reviewer ranked for their effectiveness.

Figure 3.9 User Communities and General Resources Dedicated to Open Source in Education

Resource	Location	Notes/Guidance
K–12 Open Source Wiki	http://wiki.k12opensource.com/	An open-source wiki that brings together users in a free space to share resources and ideas.
K–12 Open Technologies	http://www.k12opentech.org/	A space funded by IBM, Pearson, and others, K–12 Open Technologies seeks to promote and support the use of open-source software, instructional materials, and hardware. Articles, blogs, and software links are all available through this site.
Open Options	http://www.netc.org/openoptions/index.html	Created by the Northwest Regional Education Laboratory, this site links users to a variety of resources to help them make good decisions when pursuing open sources K–12 options.
California Learning Resource Network	http://www.clrn.org	A search and resource distribution spot, the CLRN was established to help California educators shift to digital resources once the state's textbook funding was reduced.
Classroom 2.0	http://www.classroom20.com/	A Ning Network created by Steve Hargadon, Classroom 2.0 is a great spot for teachers interested in using Web 2.0 tools to advance their classroom practice.
Future of Education	http://www.futureofeducation.com	Another great resource from Steve Hargadon, this page is treasure chest of his interviews with leading educators on topics related to the future of public education.

For live links to this software, go to **http://www.digitallearningforallnow.com,** click on the "Digital Resources" button, select the appropriate chapter from the drop-down menu, and enter the password **D L F A N** (all uppercase).

With all of this, you see here only a fraction of the available content. So, as soon as teachers find out about this great stuff, they are all going to stampede to the web and toss their textbooks out the window, right? Not so fast. Unfortunately, it appears that despite the obvious advantages, overcoming the safety and comfort of the textbook is going to be a slow to market generational process. Steve Hargadon, the emerging technologies chair for the International

Society for Technology in Education and the author of "Educational Networking: The Important Role Web 2.0 Will Play in Education," is a passionate supporter of open source at just about every level. He says that he sees the majority of open-source successes coming only when they are not replacing established habits with regrettably minimal progress elsewhere (personal communication, August 16, 2011).

Six Strategies to Get Started

The power of the status quo is a wonder to behold. I recently provided a professional development session for the faculty of a new magnet school that was to be completely digital. On the first day of training, I was astonished to see stacks of textbooks in the middle of the conference table. Even with all of their available technology, it just never occurred to them to start without a textbook. The next chapter will explore more systemically this inertia of rest, as well as organizational levers that can be pressed to overcome it, but I will close here with six easy-to-start local strategies that target the end of the print textbook. While few have the will to dump all texts at once, I have found that successfully replacing textbooks with digital resources over time is the most reliable and tangible strategy for initiating the transition to digital learning for all.

Figure 3.10 Supporting Strategies for a Transition to Open-Source Instructional Materials

Instructional Materials Change Strategy Review	
1. Set an explicit goal to get out of the textbook business	Through a collaborative planning process, create and commit to a time-specific goal that schedules replacement of texts over a five-year window. Use the Good to Great example of Walgreens and the move to get out of the luncheonette business as your working model (Collins, 2001). Start this process with a schedule of courses where you know you have willing teachers and then build the momentum moving forward.
2. Support the pioneers	Look for, develop, incentivize, and support volunteer teachers who want to take an existing textbook-based course and convert it to a digitally supported one. Treat digital resource pioneers differently from their textbook-bound peers. Celebrate digital resource champions. Talk about the future and the need to prepare kids for their lives and learning beyond school and share examples and success from your most engaging digital resource courses.

(Continued)

Figure 3.10   (Continued)

Instructional Materials Change Strategy Review	
3. **Stop the madness**	Never allow a new course to start without using open-source materials and software as a foundation.
4. **Make it a policy**	Educate your board about the wisdom and value of using digital, open-source instructional materials. Encourage them to create a policy that makes it harder to buy texts and facilitates the use of electronic materials.
5. **Hard-wire the curriculum-revision process**	Just like you should never allow a new course to start with a text, every time you commit resources to revising a curriculum document, there should be concurrent processes to realign course goals to support 21st century skills and course materials that are digital and open source.
6. **Bang the drum**	As leaders and administrators, take every opportunity to speak about the importance of this change, and never fail to demonstrate and model how these resources are a better and less expensive choice then their print alternatives.

CHAPTER SUMMARY

In this review of open source, we have learned of the movement's origins and how there is absolutely money to be saved without sacrificing quality. We examined the rise of Google and the changing perceptions of software, and how these factors have improved the market conditions. After a review of strategies for moving productivity software, we turned our attention to instructional materials. After looking at the wealth of resources available, we looked at the dangers of retrofitting and then reviewed all of the resources that are available in the market. We closed with six strategies that will create progress toward the ultimate goal of a digital and standards-aligned learning environment. There will be struggles along the way, and my experience is that there are three major barriers that are consistently the cause. Our next chapter will explore the origins of these barriers and what we can do to overcome them.

4

Overcoming Barriers to Success

Strategies for Defeating the Inertia of Print and Other Blocking Forces

Unwavering Faith

In Chapter 1, I made a reference to Jim Collins's (2001) admonition that effective leaders must be able to "confront the brutal facts." It is instructive that he pairs this difficult advice with the companion inspirational attribute of "unwavering faith that you can and will prevail in the end" (p. 13). Collins's research clearly shows that organizational transformations simply do not happen unless those responsible for leadership remain steadfastly optimistic about the future, even in the face of serious turmoil.

This delicate balance of grim truth with positive forward energy captures the perfect tone for this chapter. The reality is that change is hard for some on an individual level, and for most on an organizational one. As Ronald Heifetz and Donald Lauri (1997) have observed, the more complex the adaptive changes involved, the harder this process is and the greater the test for the organization's leadership. But in the midst of this challenge, we need to keep faith that success is possible and take courage from all of those school leaders who have demonstrated that it can be done. In these pages, I will help you face the truth of certain behavior patterns and mental paradigms that stand as barriers for school leaders who want to lead this 21st century transformation in their schools. Having exposed them, however, we will follow Collins's advice and stay positive and review numerous practical options for breaking them down. Together, we can confront the barriers and overcome them.

The Pareto Principle: The Power of Focus

Whenever getting from one point to another is the theme, the ability to achieve clarity on where it is you want to get to stands as the single most important determining factor of success. I have seen this truism play out in my personal and professional life time and time again. Over the last twenty years, in my consulting work, I have applied the logic and focusing power of the Pareto principle on hundreds of occasions. In the organizational contexts that I work in, my application of the principle demonstrates that in any process, a few root causes or issues are responsible for the vast majority of the results of that process. Do those things well, or eliminate the defects that are ruining them, and your organizational performance will take care of itself.

Originally observed by Italian economist Wilfred Pareto and implemented by the pioneers of quality control Joseph Juran, W. E. Deming, and others, the Pareto principle became known as the 80/20 rule or the "law of the vital few" ("Pareto Principle," n.d.). For a school-setting example, consider that, to be effective, a team seeking to reduce discipline referrals in a high school must begin with the reality that 80 percent of all those incidents can be attributed 20 percent of the student body. If they look further, they will discover that in that data subset, there are a few dysfunctional behaviors that account for the majority of the referrals. The law of the vital few recognizes that 80 percent of this improvement problem is locked up in a small group of behaviors in a limited group of students. If you can get those kids the help they need to improve their behavior, then your impact on the overall discipline problem you sought to improve will be great.

If you instead focus on extraneous causes that have nothing to do with this group of students, you might create terrific solutions, but the impact will be small in comparison. I have never known an instance of important organizational design decision making when adherence to the Pareto principle did not improve the outcome. Subsequently, when looking at barriers that can constrict progress in a 1:1 transition, I am going to focus on what I have found to be the "vital few" barriers in this process: issues related to control, expectations, and processes based on a belief that we can only afford one-size-fits-all strategies, and policies and decisions related to risk management. It has been my experience that targeting these roadblocks gives schools that want to move to 1:1 the greatest chance for a successful transition.

Barrier 1: It's All About Control—Part A: Curriculum and Instruction

History Repeats Itself

To label "control concerns" as only a vital barrier to change is to understate its importance in our narrative. The notion of control, or more specifically the fear and anxiety associated with losing it, could easily be written as the central theme of the information age story as a whole. This is not a new historical precedent. There was a similar wave of social upheaval when Gutenberg's press and the mass-produced printed page made the sharing of ideas and information easier six hundred years ago. Especially in medieval Europe, knowledge and control of it was power, tantamount to speaking for God. Those in positions of authority during the 16th century were wary of the widespread ability to decode and reason made possible by more egalitarian access to the printed word (Jukes, 2005). Instead of relying on a central authority for information, people could access knowledge on their own, thus undermining the power of those who sought to control both knowledge and its influence on the social order. The findings of people like Galileo and Copernicus did not fit nicely into the known worldview at the time, and the resulting angst of those associated with the status quo caused displacement and pain for many (Linder, 2002). This fear of losing control and power was not exclusive to the feudal European continent. It is the same reason that the Georgia Slave Code of 1848 established that teaching reading to African American slaves, current or freed, was a crime punishable by "fine and whipping" (Hotchkiss, 1848/2010).

In the printing press–driven knowledge revolution, the irritant was the spread of intellectual freedom and the challenges it caused to established authority. This social dynamic played out over hundreds of years and eventually remade the social order (Jukes, 2005). Today, the digital revolution is repeating this pattern. In our context, it is more than just being able to access a new idea in a book; it is the ready availability of all of the world's known information in real time. This hyper-information dynamic is causing familiar disruptions to any institution or practice that is grounded on the assumption that its mastery of a body of knowledge is its primary source of value. Travel agents, stockbrokers, information operators—it is not difficult to find a profession or segment of the economy that has not been profoundly impacted by the opening of the digital information doors.

People in these roles could once depend on their control of important information as a guarantee of future employment and status. Those that are still in business have come to realize that to remain viable, they must provide value and service beyond the facts. It is no longer enough to just know something; you must be able to do something valuable with that information. In essence, information-dependent professionals have had to raise their game to increase the level of sophistication of what they provide or else face certain extinction. The impact of these recent changes will be no less important to our own social order. And, amazingly, instead of requiring centuries of development, they have played out in just the last thirty years—a compression of history worthy of Moore's Law.

Instructional Control Barrier Strategy 1: Redefine the Role of the Teacher

Similar to other professions, teachers and professors have enjoyed a certain status that was conferred based on their mastery of the content of their subject matter. Certainly, in a secondary school classroom, this authority was rarely challenged, but as mobile access to information has grown, you can see where this is headed. When any student can fact-check or challenge a teacher's position on any topic, the classroom dynamics shift, and teacher's traditional roles are challenged. Much like when access to print shifted the power structure from the clergy to the reader, access to information is shifting the classroom power from the teacher to the learner (Jukes, 2005). Similar to their commercial peers, educators who once defined their value as knowledge gatekeepers, those who controlled academic information access, now must find a way to articulate their value beyond just what needs to be known.

This need for a new vision of the teacher's role is most bluntly articulated by tireless open-source and digital education advocate

Dr. David Thornburg when he says, "Any teacher that can be replaced by a computer, deserves to be" (personal communication, August 5, 2011). Engagement, inspiration, guidance, mentorship, and caring are the uniquely human contributions that teachers must combine with their knowledge to remain relevant. This is why MIT has created the OpenCourseWare project where they post course materials online for free. The point made is that they recognize that a student can find the information anywhere. By giving materials away, MIT is emphasizing that their value is found distinctively in what they teach students to do with the facts they learn. MIT believes it is the "dynamic classroom interactions" that define an MIT education (MIT OpenCourse Ware, n.d.).

Helping teachers think reflectively about what this new classroom role looks like and allowing them to define it through inquiry is an effective approach. This models a teaching practice suitable to this environment and gives educators a sense of control over the construction of their own future as a balance to the loss they are facing in their traditional settings. If teachers are given the time and resources they need to think about this topic, they are able to sense the shifting foundations and become part of the change process. Give them models, read materials, look to teachers in your own districts who are using problem- or inquiry-based teaching, and start building a vision of an engaged learning environment. We will explore these elements more completely in the next chapter, but at this point, Strategy 1 for overcoming control barriers in the classroom is to lead teachers through a redefinition of control to embrace the use of information and self-directed learning.

REFLECTION/STUDY QUESTION

What are the most important indicators of success of classroom settings that embrace self-directed learning? What are the advantages and disadvantages of this approach? What skills do teachers need to thrive in this environment, and what structures do you have in place to help them get there?

Instructional Control Barrier Strategy 2: Replace the Textbook

There is some irony that the textbook, the primary artifact of the Gutenberg knowledge revolution, has become a problematic barrier to opening up the classroom learning environment to digital information resources. The textbook is representative of control in this setting because it so perfectly fits with the narrative that defines a traditional classroom paradigm. We can summarize the founding assumptions this way:

- There is a defined and finite body of knowledge that students need to learn in several discrete content areas, and school is the place where you must go to learn them.
- In these areas, the classroom teacher is the designated expert, and she dictates the flow of information and the pace of learning.
- The primary information source for this process is a book that provides the neatly defined boundaries of knowledge and direction.

This is the classic factory-model school design. We control the dispensing of information, the classroom, and the clock so we can keep things moving. Even though we ended the last chapter with specific strategies to help move the textbook from center stage, it requires repeating here: A learning environment that is fluid and responsive demands informational and instructional sources that are fluid as well. As long as the textbook is allowed to dominate the classroom landscape, it will be difficult to create a learning environment that models the world outside of school.

To replace the textbook as the primary resource, we must get beyond the walls of the school. All around us, we see the crowdsourcing phenomenon; knowledge is accumulating on webpages, in wikis, on YouTube, in blogs, and the list goes on. As I described in the last chapter, the resources available are extraordinary and undeniable; all you have to do is look. The U.S. history resource collection we undertook in the summer of 2011 is an example of this, and your district can do the same. Set aside some professional time, have a specific collection goal—a project, unit, or course—and then pair teachers up to do the research and harvesting. Combine an advocate of the process with a resistor and set them to looking for resources together. The abundance and variety of what is out there can be a persuasive argument for how the center of gravity for materials and knowledge has shifted from the front of classroom to what is available on behalf of the entire academic community. Control Barrier Strategy 2 is use the open-source instructional materials outlined in Chapter 3 to make digital resources the focus of the classroom knowledge base.

REFLECTION/STUDY QUESTION

The textbook is a powerful representative artifact of a control mentality. Approved by the board and dispensed by the teacher, the textbook helps to clearly define the parameters of learning. What would your community's reaction be to a stated goal to get out of the textbook business? How amenable to your high school faculty be to the idea of "open phone" tests? Listen carefully to the reactions. To what extent are stated objections based on control and mindset factors rather than the ultimately solvable problems of material quality and appropriateness?

Instructional Control Barrier Strategy 3: Recognize That All Content Is Not Created Equal

One of the control issues that keeps the current instructional model locked in place is the total amount of declarative knowledge that we expect teachers to impart to students in their limited time with them. Whenever I work with teachers to encourage them to use inquiry processes in their classrooms, their reactions are consistent: We would love to do this but we just do not have the time. The reality is that over the last fifty years, the amount of stuff we expect kids to learn has gone up dramatically, but the time allotted for it has not increased at all. It is time to stop the madness.

Certainly, there is a body of knowledge that serves as a day-to-day foundation of basic citizenship, but the amount of knowledge that passes for the minimum in the eyes of each content area's standards is a residue of a just-in-case curriculum mentality, as in, we have to teach it "just in case" a student might need it at some point in his life. At one point, when we had no traveling access to knowledge, this was a good strategy, but we now live in a "just in time" world. What we are left with is an impossible weight of content without connection or context and no ability to explore deep meaning within one of the areas that hold interest. The current reality of standardized testing that places a high value on this type of knowledge does little to relive that pressure.

To break down this barrier, we must face the reality that all content is not created equal. As Grant Wiggins and Jay McTighe (2005) have helped to highlight with their *Understanding by Design* framework and the surrounding discussion of the "Expert Blind Spot," it is time to make the difficult choices about what truly needs to be retained and understood, and to separate that from what students should merely be aware of. Districts can take this first step locally by releasing the pressure of the content overload through the application of the Pareto principle to curriculum content standards.

To accomplish this, lay out all of the just-in-time goals and objectives from a given course or content area. Work with your curriculum team to sort through the standards and rank them from most to least critical. To guide the deliberations, use the frame of reference for stratification suggested by Wiggins and McTighe (2005) in their *Understanding by Design* framework. They ask that learning goals be sorted (in descending value) as to whether they are worth covering, teaching well, or understanding.

REFLECTION/STUDY QUESTION

How tied to the calendar and clock is your curriculum-implementation process? Is following a pacing guide more important than mastering a few critical concepts? How would a shift from "just in case" to "just in time" be perceived by teachers and curriculum writers in your district or school?

By assigning goals for learning based on long-term value, this framework assists curriculum writers in separating items according to importance and creates room within the curriculum framework for the important skill work that we will explore in the next chapter. The need for this work is starting to gain traction on a variety of different levels. My own state of Connecticut worked to prioritize all of the new Common Core State Standards in math and language arts before releasing them to the public for curriculum-development purposes. Going through this process helps to shift the focus from just in case to just in time and provides teachers with the space they need to do the most important things well while streamlining or eliminating the delivery of content that is less important.

Barrier 1: It's All About Control—Part B: Access and Equipment

Control as a Foundation of the IT Enterprise

Continuing on the same theme but shifting from the classroom, it might be unexpected that controlling behaviors among your technology support staff would be a barrier to a 1:1 transition. While you

Figure 4.1 Instructional Control Barrier Strategies Review

1. Rethinking the Teacher's Role	Engage your teachers in a collaborative discovery process that seeks to redefine the teacher's role in an information age classroom. As a professional community, how will you embrace the ready access to information to increase engagement and inquiry in your learning settings?
2. Replace the Textbook	The textbook reinforces the single-point-of-control approach to classroom learning. Replacing the textbook with multiple and varied electronic resources helps to diversify the learning environment and model real-world learning resources.
3. All Content Is Not Created Equal	Revising curriculum to reflect priorities and importance can create the time and flexibility required to allow teachers to use a wider variety of resources and teaching methods.

would think that getting everyone technology would make technology professionals happy, we need to remember what the implications of this move are. An entire generation of IT folks have been hired and trained primarily to keep the equipment and network running. This is a reasonable objective, and as the majority of issues causing downtime are related to human error, it follows that it is easy for a "protect the equipment and network from the users" mindset to develop. Add to this the fact that educational IT departments are rarely overstaffed and it is easy to see how the idea of opening the system to the entire district population would be off-putting. If your IT folks already think they are at the service limit and you propose adding 75 percent more users, it might be wise to notify them of your plan through an e-mail.

A fear of BYOD-implementation complications among IT professionals is often built on faulty assumptions that are associated with their fears of increased technology usage within their communities. Regardless of the reasons, never forget your IT staff is critical to your BYOD and 1:1 success. The earlier you can involve them and get them working on planning and preparing for the possibilities of an all-digital system, the better. Hopefully, the reason they selected this as a career is that they are interested in technology and believe in its worth, and now they get to bring these amazing tools to a larger audience. Make sure the focus remains on how we are going to make this work rather than wallowing in despair over the anticipated problems. Then, working with your IT staff, you can work with the following technology control strategies.

Technology Control Barrier Strategy 1: Support Your Own

One of the faulty assumptions regarding BYOD is that given the way we have always run IT support, you may be assuming that your IT staff will be on the hook for supporting all of the machines whether the district owns them or not. When an IT department is used to controlling all of the devices in the district's care, the idea of dramatically expanding that number is certain to blow a few minds. Happily, in successful BYOD installations, students or faculty members that bring their own equipment need to agree that they will support their own devices.

District personnel should only support district machines. Some districts provide assistance for first-time network log-ins, but after that, the users are on their own. Ensuring your device is in good working order and making good choices to keep it that way is part of the responsibility and privilege of being able to use you own device for educational purposes. If this is managed well, it is actually possible that in high-response BYOD districts, the number of supported machines would go down. This occurs because as more and more users take advantage of the opportunity to employ a personal device that they can control and customize, the burden of use on school district–owned machines is reduced.

Technology Control Barrier Strategy 2: Five-Minute Rule

As a possible further reduction of IT service exposure, with the focus on the browser and cloud-based data storage like Apple's iCloud or Amazon's Cloud Drive, BYOD support staff can use immediate reimaging of district devices as a strategy when there are user problems. When data are stored on the cloud and there is no loss of local data when a drive is wiped, it is faster to simply do that and start over than it is to go through the steps to isolate and remediate unknown problems. BYOD districts adopt the *five-minute rule*: If a tech can't solve the problem if five minutes or less, the drive is wiped, and the user starts over. Although data is saved, the prospect of a reimage is a powerful incentive for users to be mindful of device management and avoid the circumstances that would generate the need for one.

Technology Control Barrier Strategy 3: Leverage Student Expertise

Additionally, forward-thinking districts have turned to students to help them with basic user support. My wife's school, Regional

School District No. 6 (Wamogo High School) has employed a student tech team for years to provide support and help-desk functions. In the Riverside Unified School District in California, Technology Director Jay McPhail (2011) says that with 10,000 devices in use in the district, his students provide 90 percent of the needed tech support. Combined, these factors can save time, shift the burden of device support to the user, and allow IT staff to focus on the network-maintenance and network-capacity issues that support everyone.

Technology Control Barrier Strategy 4: Attack the Damage Myth

Another faulty fear-driving assumption that is made by IT departments is that current rates of damage, theft, and required repair will rise in parallel with the number of users. In a setting where students do not own devices, the inflicted destruction on district hardware is often frequent and upsetting. The more the district tries to lock them down and control access to them, the more enticing a target they seem to make. Any technician that has replaced missing mouse-balls, swapped out a broken CD/DVD disk drive, or picked gum out of a keyboard can testify to this. If a tech is spending ten hours a week on this task in support of 250 machines, how much more effort will be required when that number is 2,500?

Something interesting happens, however, when students have control over a device that is solely their own: they become responsible stewards of the equipment. This is not a faint philosophical hope. In Maine, where there are 70,000 laptops deployed in their well-established Apple 1:1 program, the devices are controlled but not owned by the student and the damage/loss rate is less than 4 percent (Goodman, 2005). Returning to Riverside Unified in California, a district where 70 percent of the students are on Free and Reduced Lunch, Jay McPhail (2011) says in his program where 10,000 BYOD and school-provided devices are completely controlled and owned by the learners, the rate is 1 percent. This statistic is a perfect example of how a shift in control, from the district to the learner, can make an incredible difference in how a resource is used in school. Similar to the shift in classroom focus from the teacher to the student that we will discuss in the next chapter, engagement and empowerment can help bridge the gap to learning in the 21st century.

Figure 4.2   Technology Control Barrier Strategies Review

1. Support Your Own	District IT staff only support those machines that are provided by the schools. Users who bring their own agree to support their own devices.
2. Five-Minute Rule	With data storage in the cloud, technicians adopt a "five-minute rule." If the problem cannot be solved in less than five minutes, drives will be reimaged, and the user starts over.
3. Leverage Student Expertise	Districts train and use student volunteers to support district users.
4. Attack the Damage Myth	Review the data regarding the damage and loss rates involved in student ownership and BYOD settings. Demonstrate the evidence that increased student ownership reduces damage and loss.

REFLECTION/STUDY QUESTION

What does the role that ownership of equipment and pride in one's own work play in shaping a student's self-image? Have you seen instances where students who you might not have believed could act responsibly rose to the occasion and did so when given the opportunity? How might you capture those examples for use in advocating for BYOD in your technology department and community?

Barrier 2: One Size Fits All

The second Pareto principle barrier to a BYOD and 1:1 transition is the time-honored ethic of "one size fits all." Born out of the school-efficiency factory model and then entrenched by an earnest yearning for equitable treatment of all students, this mental model is as set in ideological cement as any in the public school community. Providing textbooks? They will all be the same version. Reading a story in English? I'll bet you all have the same one. Credits required for graduation? It's the one number no matter which student is asking. Attendance policy, schedule of classes, homework requirements, or in any of the literally thousands of other examples, we have come to be conditioned that the only fair thing to do is to ensure that everyone has the same materials and the same experiences.

One-Size-Fits-All Barrier Strategy 1: Equity Is Not Synonymous With Sameness

The first strategy for breaking down this barrier is to state emphatically that we cannot confuse equity and equality of opportunity with doing the same thing for every student. These two concepts are not as connected as you would think. Especially when it comes to the way students learn, equal access and opportunity does not have to mean the same instructional prescription for every student. In an era where a consumer can customize sneakers, jeans, playlists, and burgers, it does not seem like a stretch to want a little individualization in the teaching and learning process.

I have seen this reality play out in my own family. As teachers, my wife and I both knew when our two boys were young how important writing performance was going to be to their success as students. My oldest is a visual learner like his mom; my youngest, a logical, language-driven sequential thinker. When the elder was first getting started, to add depth to his writing, we encouraged him, with the support of his teacher, to draw what he was going to write first and then translate those images into words. For the young one, the traditional outline and organizational strategies worked just fine. Today, our first is a journalism major, and the second a fine writer in his own right.

It would have made no sense for my youngest son's teacher to insist that he draw what he was going to write before composing, just as it would have been a waste for the older one to start with outlines. Equity for us in this situation meant the outcome. We wanted them both to be good writers but understood it would take different pathways to get them there. Years of research on differentiated instruction support this approach (Block & Paris, 2008). We need to emphasize the understanding that specialized, sometimes differentiated processes that use varied resources are the only way to ensure universal levels of elevated achievement. When we value high standards of achievement as the most important indicator of equity, we allow for customized learning. By giving students and teachers access to a world of information and resources, 1:1 helps make that possible on a much larger scale than available print materials could ever do.

One-Size-Fits-All Barrier Strategy 2: Celebrate the Power of Differentiation

Just as we explored how the move to the browser has made the use of different equipment less of an equity issue, it is time we recognize the significant potential in digitally aligning materials and lessons with each student's needs. This ability to use technology to customize and differentiate materials and instruction is one of the most powerful advantages of a digital learning environment. Through this customization, teachers can become much more adept at meeting students where they are and advancing their achievement. We know each learner is an individual with unique interests and needs. As such, it only makes sense that our goal should be to align as much as possible the resources each learner uses with these individualities.

With the digital tools of a 1:1 classroom, teachers can enlist students in assisting with their own differentiation. The most important thing we can do for our students is to empower them to be their own customized lesson designers. Giving students control over what role they want to play as content creators or allowing them to choose the format and audience for their work are all ways to engage them in as self-directed learners. Project-based or problem-based learning where teachers give students wide choices about how best to pursue their learning are time-tested strategies to support this approach. Whether by design or serendipity, like my story of writing success with my children, I know you have examples of how teachers used differentiated instruction or personalized learning to reach students in their care.

These stories of student success are very powerful, and every school has them. One of the most effective strategies for breaking down the barrier of one size fits all is to continuously celebrate stories of when not following that maxim benefitted children in your school. By consistently calling attention to those teachers and student results, especially when technology was involved, you will be helping to create a new value of customized learning. The more we can customize in the name of shared high achievement, the better the results for all our students.

Figure 4.3 One-Size-Fits-All Barrier Strategies Review	
1. **Equity Is Not Sameness**	Delinking the concepts of equity and sameness of approach are foundational to raising achievement for all.
2. **Celebrate Differentiation**	Find and celebrate examples of teachers using different methods of teaching to support student achievement.

REFLECTION/STUDY QUESTION

When was the last time you were in a situation where you were forced to accept a solution or product that was not aligned with your expectations? Would it have been more effective if the circumstances were different? How would the increased ability or willingness to adjust to conditions and meet learners where they are improve your school's or district's ability to support student achievement?

Barrier 3: Risk Aversion

You Can't Boil the World

When our first son was born, in the weeks after we brought him home, my wife was taking particular care to disinfect and sanitize anything that could come into contact with the baby. In one of my son's early appointments with our pediatrician, my wife was telling him about her disinfecting efforts. The late, great Dr. Joe Curi looked over his spectacles as only a wise country doctor can and said, "You know Wendy, we can't boil the world." The third barrier that blocks a move to 1:1 is a risk-averse culture that seeks to "boil the world" of the information age to shield all of us from anything in it that might potentially cause us harm. Obviously, just as in household life, some common-sense safety and prevention activity is appropriate, but going ten extra miles does not necessarily make anyone safer and can actually cause educational harm.

For example, most would agree that basic virus/worm protection and the blocking of obvious pornography sites are welcome and expected security measures that should be taken. But when we take this defensive step to its extreme and lock down network access tight to prevent any possible problem, we create a situation where productive work is prevented as well. In doing so, we value security over learning, protection over preparation, and ultimately help to ensure that students are not adequately prepared for the world in which they will soon live and work. The best place to look for evidence of this outlook is in the structures that frame most school-based interaction with the digital world: the acceptable-use policy.

Risk-Aversion Strategy 1:
Move From Zero to Acceptable Risk

Most districts operate on a zero-risk frame of reference and define acceptable use through the negative, a listing of what students *should not* do with the technology. You can't use your phone, you cannot get on Facebook, and so on. First, let's look at the concept of zero risk. As a former board of education member, I know that boards are famously intolerant of surprises. So, when administrators talk about network security and filtering practices, they tend to oversell them on how secure and safe their infrastructure is. By doing this, we imply to the outside world that our combination of locking and blocking is keeping all children completely safe from any outside risk. As any IT professional will tell you, this is a false assumption.

No matter how brilliant your security, there is always a risk. Some student or some person who seeks to do the district harm will always be able to find a way to cause trouble if that is his goal. The discussion with boards has to be about manageable or acceptable risk. What is the optimal level of security that will both prevent casual users from getting into trouble while at the same time providing enough flexibility to allow for the accomplishment of productive work? The first strategy is to just be honest about the nature of the beast and start talking about the issues in realistic terms that reflect reality.

Risk-Aversion Strategy 2:
Focus on Responsible Use, Not Prohibiting Use

When thinking of the idea of risk, it is helpful to remember Truth 2 from our first chapter: If our mission is to prepare children for success in the 21st century, it makes sense that they are going to need to work in a preparatory phase in an environment that has some of the same characteristics as the one in which they will eventually work and learn. Shawn Nutting, the technology director of the Trussville, Alabama, school district where they recently changed their filtering policies to allow access to blogs, YouTube, and social networking says,

> We are known in our district for technology, so I don't see how you can teach kids 21st century values if you are not teaching them digital citizenship and appropriate ways of sharing and using everything that is available on the web. (Kennedy Manzo, 2009)

In other words, it is better to prepare students by teaching them how make judgments and decisions about what has value than it is to make these decisions for them. This begins by setting clear rules and expectations, essentially creating a set of standards for what is acceptable and what is not, and then using adult supervision to ensure that the standards and practices are effectively followed in the learning environment. As mentioned, the collective instinct on how to accomplish this has been to state the directives in the negative, to define the parameters of acceptable use around what we want to prevent.

It is common for districts to have similar policies for adults and require that both adults and students sign off on their acknowledgement of the policy at least once and sometimes annually. What is interesting about these policies is they seek to outlaw all known behavior that is not currently deemed acceptable even if there is a possibility for a legitimate use within these parameters. Chat rooms, instant messaging, and social networking are prime examples of this. They also seek to block all offensive content, often tangling appropriate instructional sites in with much less acceptable materials. Additionally, they seek to ban a student from further use if she habitually breaks the rules. Can you imagine a district ever telling a student, "You have lost four books, no more books for you!"

Another component to consider is the rapidly changing nature of technology itself. New devices, applications, and services are being created at such a rate that any attempt to explicitly ban something are quickly swamped by alternatives or new devices that make the "old" policy language irrelevant. How could the Children's Internet Protection Act (CIPA) have anticipated social networking or text messaging when it was being considered in 2001–2003? Consider that Twitter did not exist when CIPA was written. Founded in 2006, Twitter's army of users now post about 200 million tweets per day or roughly 1 billion tweets per week (Panzarino, 2011). Do we want to rewrite policy every time a new technology is created?

Provide Models and Emphasize the Positive

The question, then, is how to create a policy balance that allows for access and timeliness, but at the same time provides for an adequate level of protection from dangerous content. Experience dictates that a successful policy intervention in this area would need to meet the following criteria:

- clear definitions and standards for what the community believes is acceptable content and what skill outcomes are valued by the community,
- a process for helping determine what fits the standards and under what conditions,

- enough flexibility to work in a rapidly changeable technology environment, and
- easy sharing to assist members of the community in understanding what schools are doing and why they are using the processes that they are.

The ultimate goal is to create a policy that can act as an effective behavior guideline while at the same time helping educators teach students about what is appropriate. When districts try to meet these guidelines only by defining the negative, they encourage an all or nothing interpretation. All of these sites are bad or anything in this category is off limits. Life, learning, and the real world are rarely so cleanly segmented as to allow simple use guidance that keeps out all the evil while allowing all of the good. How would one study art history, for example, if a total ban on images of the female breast was in place? Probably a third of all baroque European art would be off limits. Other topics that get swept up in the blocks are as varied as sociology, religion, and anatomy. Just blocking an item without context does as much to prevent learning of appropriate topics than it does prevent bad what it is intended to stop.

Use Goals and Standards

The bottom line here is that it makes no sense to use a blocking sledgehammer when a scalpel is the best tool for the job. This principle should apply to acceptable use and other technology guideline policies. Policies might begin by actually outlining the purpose of technology use in the first place, like developing 21st century skills that will help students succeed in life and work beyond school. This approach allows districts to define acceptable use in the positive form. This sets the tone by leading with the most important things that students are supposed to do rather than trying to list all of the millions of things they should not. For example, after an opening statement to take care of a couple of general legal provisions, a district can then go on to define what is acceptable and purpose aligned by tying behavior to specific goals. The sample in Figure 4.4 is excerpted from a model we provide to districts who use EDUCATION CONNECTION's Center for 21st Century Skills courses. Each bullet corresponds to one of our recommended 21st century skills.

In a district setting, adults could sign a similar framework in which they promise to only use technology in support of activities

Figure 4.4   Sample Policy Introduction

Employees and students should be aware that the Agency may monitor usage of electronic resources by individuals and that all electronic resources have been provided to employees and students of EDUCATION CONNECTION to support the business and educational purposes of the Agency. Employees and staff of the Agency are responsible for ensuring that they understand and follow this policy, and I promise that my use of the Internet and digital resources for learning in our district will be used to ensure that I legally

- use real-world digital and other research tools to access, evaluate and effectively apply information appropriate for authentic tasks;
- work independently and collaboratively to solve problems and accomplish goals;
- communicate information clearly and effectively using a variety of tools/media in varied contexts for a variety of purposes;
- demonstrate innovation, flexibility, and adaptability in thinking patterns, work habits, and working/learning conditions;
- effectively apply the analysis, synthesis, and evaluative processes that enable productive problem solving; and
- value and demonstrate personal responsibility, character, cultural understanding, and ethical behavior.

that seek to encourage these same skills in their students. For those that think it is naïve to believe that this simple positive statement would be enough to stop abhorrent behavior, remember, there is no such thing as anonymity on the Internet. All behavior can be tracked and potentially discovered. Any obvious illegal activity would be punished as such. For the gray areas, it would be understood that any controversy or challenge to a student's use of content or materials would then have to be defended through one of these lenses.

For example, if a student had been engaged in behavior deemed inappropriate, he would have to defend what he did by making a case for how it was assisting in the achievement of one or more of the stated 21st century skills. To aid in this, a rubric for evidence and judgment is developed that would give the scoring and judgment of such infractions more structure. A sample of what this might look like is found in Figure 4.5. This rubric would make clear that the district does not and is not advocating for the illegal or indiscriminate use of technology or digital content, only that it favors the thoughtful application of same. The framework then is used to determine whether an activity was acceptable under the conditions it was applied and would be used in discipline and sanctions actions if so required.

Figure 4.5   Sample Acceptable-Use Policy Implementation Rubric

Item	Unacceptable	Marginal	Acceptable	Excellent
Legal considerations	Content or process is illegal. The student has done something or used something that is not allowed through the statutes or other existing laws (including but not limited to fair use and age appropriateness provisions).	Content or process is only marginally legal. While there may be a rationale, the student has done something or used something that can be interpreted as not allowed through the statutes or other existing laws (including but not limited to fair use and age appropriateness provisions).	Content or process is legal. There is an articulated educational rationale, and the outcome is both educationally and legally acceptable (including but not limited to fair use and age appropriateness provisions).	Content or process is clearly legal. There is an effectively articulated educational rationale, and the outcome is both educationally and legally sound with recognized impact (including but not limited to fair use and age appropriateness provisions).
Content connections	There is no plausible connection to an established curriculum goal within the district.	There is a plausible connection to an established curriculum goal within the district.	There is a reasonable connection to an established curriculum goal within the district.	There is an explicit and direct connection to an established curriculum goal within the district.
Appropriate usage	The content was not used for any appropriate application.	While some of the content was not used for an appropriate application, there is evidence that parts were.	The content was used for an appropriate application.	The entirety of the content was used for an appropriate application.

Additional advantages of this "goal and standards" approach to acceptable use are that, first, it does not legally tie the policy to any one specific technology. Subsequently, this framework not only helps to guide the use of the available technology today in the environment as it exists now, but also has the flexibility to change and adapt as technologies change with it. Second, it mirrors the same approach we all take with standards and learning outcomes in the classroom. We have a goal for good writing and a rubric that describes what it is so that a model can be apparent. This structure does the same for our technology behavior as well. Finally, this framework also helps to remind everyone why these digital tools are used in the first place. By stating the goals for learning as a policy foundation and requiring all applications of the policy to be defended through this same lens, the district helps educate and reinforce the value of the use of technology and how it is aligned with the mission of the district.

REFLECTION/STUDY QUESTION

How effective is your current acceptable-use policy, and what educational opportunities does it provide? Good policy should guide behavior but also be a foundation for framing lessons about what we expect from the choices that students make. What changes could you make to the policy frameworks in place in your district so they serve educational as well as behavioral functions?

Risk-Aversion Strategy 3: Understanding Common and Special Causes

No section that involves the issue of risk management and policy is complete without an explicit mention of the differences between common and special causes. First observed by Walter Shewart and then made famous by W. Edwards Deming in his quality studies of the 1950s and 1960s, the understanding of predictable variation of the limits of any system has become the foundation of improving every manufacturing production line ever since (Deming, 1982). Social scientists and educators who make organizational decisions based on this understanding enjoy far greater effectiveness than those that do not.

Common causes are those that are predictable, controllable, and systemic because they are caused by the system itself. For example, we decide as a society that we want students to be knowledgeable about American history; we change the public education system to require that all students take and pass that class before they can graduate. The impact of this decision is predictable; more students leave the public schools with knowledge of American history than did before we required it.

Special causes are random, unpredictable, and beyond the control of the system. Abraham Lincoln is famously noted for having taught himself to read. Should we then assume that all students should be able to teach themselves to read, and therefore no longer require reading to be taught in public schools? Of course not. We recognize Abe to be an outlier, a singular talent that we cannot generalize to the rest of the population. Schools have dealt with similar prodigies in other contexts in similar fashion. Figure 4.6 demonstrates these common cause and special cause differences.

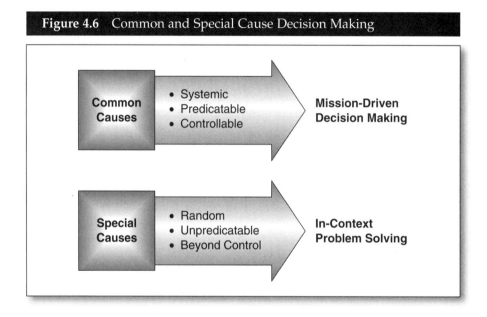

Figure 4.6   Common and Special Cause Decision Making

In a technology policy environment, what common cause and special cause understanding helps us see is that there are certain behaviors that are predictable, that we know are going to happen because they are caused or made possible by the system. Teenage boys with access to the Internet, if given the opportunity, will try at some point to see pictures of girls in various states of undress. We know this to be the case, so we take common cause, systems-based, prudent precautions to prevent this from happening. Filtering all of the district's networks for pornographic images is a good start. No surprise so far. Where we go off the rails is when we try to come up with systemic technology solutions for problems that are random or not predictable.

Think about an Abraham Lincoln–like computer genius outlier who finds a way to hack into the Pentagon's computer system. Or imagine a once-in-a-century storm that takes out the main power supply line to a school for an entire week. Unlike the obvious restrained reaction in the example of Lincoln and the question of teaching reading, what will likely happen in districts that cannot separate common from special causes is that on the next board of education agenda, we see a proposal to ban all student computer-programming instruction and a movement to eliminate web-based curriculum resources based on fear of a power outages. These reactions are not supported by system data. A learner with that kind of intellect would have taught himself programming on the Internet if he did not get the basics in school. When schools pursue these unnecessary policy actions, they almost certainly end up diverting district resources from other areas where they could do far more good. A random event is by definition unpredictable. It's like trying to create a system to consistently guess winning lottery numbers; it is not possible. When school systems make decisions based on the fear of an unpredictable and unpreventable risk, they hold the entire system hostage to that fear. Systems changes should only be made based on common cause functions that are aligned with the district goal. Technology policy and implementation is a perfect example.

Common cause problems deserve systemic reactions. Policy changes, rule adjustments, equipment purchases—in short, a strategy designed to prevent the predictable event. Special cause problems call for judgment and thoughtful single-application solutions. There is no need to change everyone's behavior and redirect resources because one random event occurred. As with the one-size-fits-all lesson from earlier in this chapter, so it is also with problem solving in technology or school management. Before you go to implement a one-size solution, be sure that you have a problem that justifies it. Knowing the difference between a common and special cause will improve your efficiency and your ability to make progress toward your stated goals.

Figure 4.7   Risk-Aversion Barrier Strategies Review

1. **Move From Zero to Acceptable Use**	Start the discussion about the realities of risk and how a true zero-risk approach would mean a complete system shutdown.
2. **Focus on Responsible Use, Not Prohibiting Use**	Shift the focus of acceptable use policy and implementation from the negative prohibition of behaviors to modeling positive applications and adherence to standards of behavior grounded on 21st century skills.
3. **Understand the Difference Between Common and Special Cause Data**	Common cause problems deserve systemic reactions. Special cause problems call for judgment and thoughtful single-application solutions.

REFLECTION/STUDY QUESTION

Have you observed incidents of common cause/special cause confusion in distric-twide decision making? What data or factors were present or missing that led to these decisions being made and implemented? What could be done to reverse or prevent this type of problem, especially as it relates to a movement to BYOD, in the future?

CHAPTER SUMMARY

In this chapter, we reviewed three of biggest barriers to implementing a BYOD, open-source, 1:1 instructional program and the associated strategies that can be used to overcome them. First, we examined issues related to control and learned the definition and many applications of the Pareto principle. We saw how this played out in control of knowledge, control of the learning process, and also its application to control of the equipment and networks. We walked through these print-based paradigms and reviewed strategies that can be used to overcome them. We then looked at how the quest for efficiency created a one-size-fits-all mentality that will be uniquely challenged in a 1:1 environment. And finally, we explored risk management, the impact of a positive policy outlook, and the differences between common and special cause problem solving. Any and all of these barriers and our responses to them will impact the pace of change we are able to create in our districts.

Regardless of the pace, this change will happen eventually. As we will explore in Chapter 6, overcoming the fear of change often comes down to how personal decisions and experiences are molded and shaped by individuals. Before we do that, though, we are going to pick up on the systems theme that we ended this chapter with. Associated with common and special cause thinking are important lessons for the type of systems thinking that will be needed to make the move to a 1:1 instructional model as effective as it has the potential to be. An analysis of those systems and how they interact form the basis of Chapter 5 of *Digital Learning for All, Now.*

PART III

Building the System

5

Systems and Measurement

Aligning Instruction, Assessment, and Support Systems With 21st Century Outcomes

Three Phases of Technology Integration

The goal of the first two sections of *Digital Learning for All, Now* was to give district leadership the tools they need to move a district from print to 1:1. If you have decided to follow that path and take this journey, congratulations! Before you leave, take some time to think about what you want your school district to look like a few years after the digital transition is complete. It would be unfortunate to put effort into planning and taking a grand trip, only to be disappointed with your destination.

To be clear, the process mechanics of moving from print to digital described in Chapters 2 and 3 are proven and effective. You will be able to finance and get to 1:1 if you follow them. The open issue is whether or not you will realize the full benefit of digital learning once every student has a device and learning is underway. Earlier, I warned about the adoption of the simple digital text as an inflexible and limited technology retrofit of the printed textbook. With significant expense and little cognitive return, that application of technology is hard to justify on a cost-value basis. Now, think of repeating that retrofitting mistake across all of the instructional and support functions of your district. The stakes are high in this game, and you only get a chance to remake a school system once in a generation; you need to get it right.

As a way to put this into context, consider the historical patterns of change that occur when technology rolls through a market segment. In a speech in 2004, I discussed what I considered to be the three phases of technology integration. I alluded to this framework in the Chapter 3 discussion of digital textbooks. The *retrofit* is a typical Phase 1 behavior, where institutions perform the same functions in essentially the same ways that they did before technology arrived, only now they do it with a different tool. Like a bank shifting from ledgers to spreadsheets, the phone company going from rotary to touchtone, or a teacher going from overheads to PowerPoint, the retrofit is a tepid first level of integration. Because there is no significant gain in functionality, if the process ended here, these transitions would not be worth the money or effort.

In Phase 2, *reengineering*, technology allows institutions to do an enhanced version of what they used to do, but with meaningful additional services or options. The bank goes from tellers taking deposits and withdrawals to freeing the customer from banker's hours with the ATM. The phone shifts from being wired to the wall to wireless and truly portable. Research for education is unbound from the book and moves to the Internet. These advances do two things. First, they allow organizations to enable customers' greater access to their services and in doing so realize a true productivity return on their technology investment. Think of the bank that gets its customers to do the teller's work through the ATM and then charges them a fee as a thank you! The second thing it does is help build the momentum of consumer demand for the third phase, *rethinking*.

As consumers become more enamored with the idea of their own control, they reciprocate the opening of the service options with increased demand to take these trends further. As the layers add on, these new levels of empowerment granted to consumers lead eventually to a rethinking of the foundational assumptions on which the institution is constructed. With web banking, mobile banking apps, ATM cards, and cell-phone bar scanners for checkout, we have to ask, what is the role of a bank branch in an increasingly cashless society? If a person can manage their own money and has access to all of these tools, they might never walk into another bank building again. When a handheld device can do TV, Internet, e-mail, text, and calls, what does a landline phone company do? We know the answer: it goes out of business. When students can access materials and be learners from anywhere at any time, how relevant is a school that remains organized and run based on a print belief system that assumes they can't?

Figure 5.1   Three Phases of Technology Integration

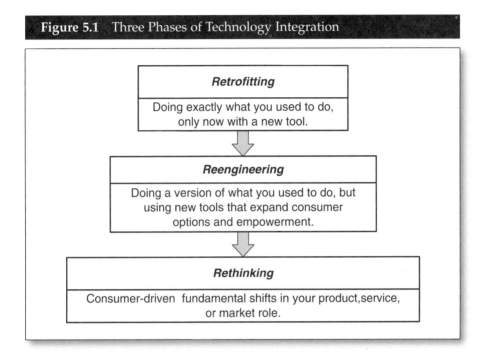

I do not believe that schools are in the same risk category as landline phone companies. There are many social and economic reasons to ensure for the foreseeable future that there will always be "brick and mortar schools," especially at the K–6 levels. What I know to be true, however, is that secondary schools are in a pitched battle to stay relevant. As young adults comprehend the world around them and the challenges that it will entail, they increasingly believe that the learning tools they are using in middle/high school are inadequate to prepare them properly for it. As we discussed in the first chapter, this perception goes beyond just not having technology because of budget concerns; it extends to outright animosity toward student and staff electronic devices with rules and policies that restrict or prohibit use completely. So as adults profess to want students to learn, they often are found enforcing rules that students believe are preventing them from doing exactly that. For teens who have phones confiscated, the 7–12 print-based school is seen as an interruption in the learning process.

Getting equipment into schools will not be enough. We must lead the discussion about what rethought schools look like in a digital age and implement the shift ourselves, before outsiders do it for us and in a way that we might not favor. How can we make these changes in a way that enhance relationships between students, teachers, and the learning environment? In the commercial world, we have seen how external market forces have driven change and remade entire industries. For schools, the process has been slower to develop because it depends on consumer empowerment for its energy. Without 1:1 access for learners, the movement is denied fuel to grow. As students get and use devices, the pressure for systems realignment will increase. If you have any doubts that this will occur, consider the current stress on higher education to adopt online learning strategies. As U.S. postsecondary enrollment grows at a pace of 2 percent per year, online postsecondary enrollment is growing at a rate ten times that (Allen, 2010). If your business is a graduate school, how do you ignore that data? The change is coming; the key is making the most of it when it arrives.

Systems of School Improvement and Their Impact on 21st Century Learning

Knowing that technology installations alone are not enough, how do we manage or undertake a rethinking process that will move us past retrofitting to rethinking in a productive way? In previous chapters, I have mentioned the work of Joseph Juran, Walter Shewart, and W. Edwards Deming. All of these men are associated with the quality sciences, and their insights regarding the impact of systems on work quality reshaped the world economy in the last half of the 20th century. As we look to redesign schools for the 21st century, we would be wise to apply their lessons learned to our own rethinking efforts.

As Deming (1982) so vividly demonstrated in his defect management simulation exercises, the key insight of systems thinking is that it is the way work is done that is the primary driver of quality produced within that system. If you build a factory whose systems are known to produce errors at a rate of 20 percent, it is pointless to blame or challenge the employees within that workplace to improve performance just by trying harder. The majority of the defects are in the process, not the employees. Every identifiable system of work is defined by a series of processes, or steps, that people take to get the work done. If you design improvements into these processes, most of the time the quality of the work improves along with them.

The same applies to schools trying to support 21st century learning for students. Just imploring teachers to "really try" to focus on 21st century skills or the Common Core State Standards and work harder to engage students while not examining how all of the processes and systems work together to support that effort is a prescription for frustration and failure. If we want educators to teach higher-order digital thinking, we need to look at how we set goals for this, how we measure student performance on those goals, how we professionally prepare teachers, what equipment we provide, and on and on. The history of school change is a litany of great ideas that were layered on top of existing systems as effort-based exhortations. These promising practices make a splash at the annual professional development day and then are largely forgotten. We cannot afford a superficial pass at rethinking systems for a 1:1 digital environment.

But, where should we start? In totality, it seems an overwhelming task. There are many variables and numerous entry points to consider. To make it manageable, we will once again turn to the Pareto principle (see Chapter 4) for guidance and focus just on the critical primary and underlying systems that support teaching and learning. These systems are the major gears of the organizational school engine that will need to be realigned with the goals of a 1:1 digital teaching and learning space to make meaningful changes occur. I believe there are eight such key systems that are most responsible for driving the focus and results of your school district.

The first four are associated primarily with the intense work that is the foundation of the teaching and learning enterprise: goal setting, instructional processes, assessment, and the leadership practices that hold them together. These are the systems of work that have the most immediate impact on the student–teacher relationship and as such will be our "top tier." Supporting these are four additional systems that include curriculum and communications, professional support, professional evaluation, and resource allocation. This chapter will provide an overview of each one of these areas, specify indicators of success for each, and provide examples from district practice for illustration purposes. Additionally, there is a parallel set of more detailed self-assessment standards on the *Digital Learning for All, Now* webpage for each of these systems. The standards guide reflective practice regarding the status of each of these indicators in your school or district. Adjusting these system gears in synchronicity with your goals for 21st century learning is the key to ensuring that your change efforts will have the desired impact on preparing students for their future.

REFLECTION/STUDY QUESTION

What is the current state of systems thinking in your district or school? One of the best ways to determine this is to be reflective about what happens when things go bad. Is the first leadership reaction to problems a search to find out who is to blame or is it to focus on what happened and how to correct it before it happens again? If "blamestorming" is your preferred problem-solving process, what can be done to shift the focus to those systems elements that are most responsible for organizational performance?

Guided Rethinking: New Assumptions and Aligned Systems

To start the process of rethinking top-tier systems, we can begin by examining the operating assumptions on which they are based. I have mentioned earlier what many before have observed: public schools are built on series of print-based and efficiency model design criteria that mold their creation. Decades of supporting or restraining legislation and policy aligned with this framework have ensured the consistent application to the degree that most American high schools are structurally indistinguishable from one another.

Driven by a textbook mindset of teaching the content "just in case," these assumptions put the spotlight on the teacher's podium and use time as the constant. With the calendar as the master, the text as the tool, and the march through forty-eight-minute periods as the core drill, students put their heads down and play the game as they grind their way to twenty-four seat-time credits. In this environment, instructional differentiation is limited because it is teacher dependent. Rigor is measured by the volume of content retained, and engagement is associated with a student's willingness to go along with all of the assumptions that frame the exercise. Variations on this theme are isolated, usually showing up as a stand-alone alternative education program for students who will not put up with these accepted practices. Seen together, these assumptions can be summarized as follows:

When students control their own devices and can work freely within the information environment, it is possible to consider what the possibilities are when one challenges these assumptions. If learning was the constant instead of time, and if mastery of competencies decided when you moved on instead of the calendar, what would the impact on school design be? With the new focus on high national standards for all, if a student can master those standards in ten years instead of thirteen, does she really need to stay that long? And if it takes me fifteen, but I get it right before I leave, is it more important that I have the skills I need or that I finished on the same schedule as everyone else? Instead of a content-driven rigor standard, replace it with a balanced skill and content approach that uses 21st century assessments to gauge not only what was learned but also how well it was used. Allow learners to take ownership of their learning, and measure engagement by the quality of their work, not by how compliant they were as they passed through the years.

Figure 5.2 Foundational Assumptions of Print-Based Schools

Old Assumptions
Time is the constant
Content mastery, just in case
Standardized instruction
Rigor means "how much?"
Print resources
One size fits all
Experts have authority and control
Engagement is compliance

Figure 5.3 shows our rethought systems assumptions set side by side with their predecessors.

Figure 5.3 New Assumptions of 1:1 Schools

Old Assumptions	New Assumptions
Time is the constant	**Learning** is the constant
Content mastery, just in case.	**Content** and skills balance, just in time
Standardized instruction	**Standards** of achievement
Rigor means "how much?"	**Rigor** means "how well?"
Print resources	**Digital** resources
One size fits all	**One size fits one**
Experts have authority and control	**Learners** have dignity and ownership
Engagement is compliance	**Engagement** is purpose-driven focus

REFLECTION/STUDY QUESTION

What is your reaction to these new assumptions? How many are you comfortable with, and which need further exploration? Which are more troubling or exciting than others? What would you predict would be the impact of these frames of reference on the way your current school processes work?

When systems redesign is pushed through these lenses, the outcomes can begin to take different shapes and ultimately become more responsive to 21st century learning needs. Beyond the obvious working implications of these new assumptions, one of the additional challenges of this shift is that it really cannot be implemented as a "pick and choose" exercise. Just as with the systems themselves, there are connections between all of these conceptual changes. You cannot give students digital access to resources and encourage inquiry and ownership and then not expect those evolving perspectives to grow a demand that will impact other areas of the system as well.

This is why I like the metaphor of system gears as an illustrating device in this chapter. Just as trying to change the direction or speed of one gear within an engine without doing the same to the others connected to it will have a disastrous impact, so should changing one instructional support system without concurrent adjustments to others. Why would a district invest in equipment purchasing, professional development, and curriculum improvements without explicitly tying all of those processes to one focused goal?

In fact, the better the alignment of your current system gears, the harder it should be to change just one without disrupting others. If you can freely shift the focus of one key system without having a detrimental impact on others, that is a solid indicator that your system gears are so loosely coupled that they are just freely spinning. When the key operational centers are doing whatever they want, they are wasting potential energy and not moving you ahead. Forward momentum requires organizational traction that can only be generated by system gears working together to harness the power of the district's human engine. Align and connect the systems and they will drive your organization in the direction you want to go, namely, every student being prepared for life, learning, and work in the 21st century.

Four Foundational Systems: Part 1—Focus, Focus, Focus

The four most important systems that support any classroom are the goals for learning, the methods of instruction and assessment applied in that setting, and the leadership structures that hold all of this together. It should not be surprising that two of the four first-tier systems that support a 21st century 1:1 learning environment are related to leadership, goals, and focus. Clarity of purpose has been identified again and again as the foundation of organizational effectiveness. Deming (*Out of the Crisis*, 1982), Goldratt and Cox (*The Goal*), Barker (*The Power of Vision*, 1990), Collins (*Good to Great*, 2001), Wiggins and McTighe (*Understanding by Design*, 2005) and many others have all sent the same message: You must start with the end in mind. So, we must begin the systems rethinking process by stating with great clarity what we want students to know and be able to do when they leave our schools. This should be done in mission language for the district and as specific skills for every student. With this complete, the entire district leadership structure should then spend every opportunity reinforcing its importance through consistent words and actions.

Great care should be taken to ensure that this skill-identification exercise is focused on what *students will* need, not what they used to need. As curriculum leader Heidi Hayes Jacobs (2010) asks in the introduction to her book *Curriculum 21*, "Can you honestly say that you are preparing your students for 2015 or 2020? Are you even preparing them for today?" (p. 1). Figure 5.4 demonstrates the critical needed alignment between the leadership mission at the organizational level and 21st century goals for learning at the classroom level.

Figure 5.4   Top-Tier Systems for 21st Century Learning

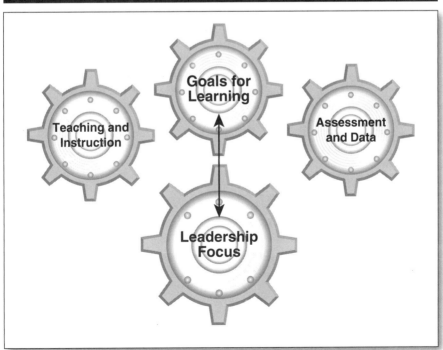

With focus as a priority, as always, we turn to Pareto principle for guidance. There are hundreds of skills and attributes that could be identified as contributing factors to 21st century success. The key is finding which of those will have the largest impact and zeroing in on them as you build the other supporting structures. If a district believes in the mission of preparing students for life, learning, and work in the 21st century as an organizational mission, then the six 21st century skills introduced in Chapter 1 can be a good foundation for skill goals at the classroom level.

Figure 5.5   EDUCATION CONNECTION's Consensus List of 21st Century Skills

1. Use real-world digital and other research tools to access, evaluate, and effectively apply information appropriate for authentic tasks.
2. Work independently and collaboratively to solve problems and accomplish goals.
3. Communicate information clearly and effectively using a variety of tools/media in varied contexts for a variety of purposes.
4. Demonstrate innovation, flexibility, and adaptability in thinking patterns, work habits, and working/learning conditions.
5. Effectively apply the analysis, synthesis, and evaluative processes that enable productive problem solving.
6. Value and demonstrate personal responsibility, character, cultural understanding, and ethical behavior.

No district that I have worked with has taken this admonition to focus core leadership and goal-setting systems more to heart than the North Salem Public Schools, in North Salem, New York. A small district in northern Westchester County, North Salem is ably led by Superintendent Dr. Kenneth R. Freeston and his assistant superintendent for curriculum and instruction, Dr. K. Michael Hibbard. During a strategic planning retreat in 2009, a collaborative team of thirty educators and citizens from across the North Salem community agreed on a new mission statement. Just fifteen words long, it was designed to capture not only the purpose of a 21st century learning organization but the focus of classroom practice as well. They succeeded brilliantly.

Figure 5.6   North Salem's Mission Statement

Engage students to continuously learn, question, define and solve problems through critical and creative thinking.

Source: Freeston and Hibbard (2009). Reprinted with permission.

You may be thinking that this is oversimplifying the process; how can anyone succeed with a mission that translates into just one instructional goal? After watching what has transpired in North Salem over the last two years, I would turn it around and ask, how can anyone succeed with more than just one? As Ken and Mike have led the systems-improvement process through a realignment with this new mission, the depth and quality of their staff's work demonstrates clearly that when powerful ideas are explored thoroughly, the end result is of greater significance to students than any mile-wide and inch-deep approach could ever hope to create.

Ken started the process by assuring his board that they would maintain their excellent testing performance, but that they would turn their improvement energies toward the mission and work to align practice with it. Then, as Mike orchestrated the unpeeling of the layers of this simply stated but incredibly complex undertaking, they have identified substantive characteristics and evidence that they believe are markers for successful student accomplishment of this mission. This has led to the codification of desired characteristics of both critical and creative thinking, elements of teaching strategies and lessons designed to support them, project-design criteria and assessment practices, and a waterfall of other systemic adjustments.

The end result is that every teacher in the district is on the way to playing a distinct role in contributing to the mission. It is clear at every level that all of the system gears are turning toward mission progress, and because they are focused on rigor and complexity of content, they are well positioned for Common Core success and any other external assessment that might come their way. North Salem is a living example that less, in the form of fewer goals, greater depth, and shared rigor, really can result in higher quality and richness of results. This is the power that focus can bring to the improvement process.

And by all indications, in the era of high-stakes accountability, when making the transition to 1:1, you are going to need all of the power that you can get. With budgets tight and millions flowing through the system, the pressure to produce results is ever present. Without clarity in terms of 21st century goals for learning, when it comes time to reflect your progress in assessment reports, you are going to have to rely on tests that don't reflect what you profess to care about in the first place. As we will discuss in the next section regarding assessment, making the transition from drill and practice testing to a balance between content and skill demonstrations can be difficult when performance expectations are only reported in the content realm. It makes no sense to defend the quality of a new model by using the results of the old. Would a bank use data on "increasing teller transactions" as a way to determine the future success of a digital banking strategy? The only way to avoid this trap is to be transparent about your goals and to articulate them clearly.

Before BYOD, and without the use of open-source materials, many districts that went to 1:1 the expensive way have been caught up in this debate. A front-page story in the September 4, 2011, *New York Times* examined the flat test scores of the Kyrene School District in Arizona (Richtel, 2011). Educators in this community asked for and received millions of extra dollars to give every student a laptop as well as an array of other technology-support devices. The additional money that had to be put on the table led to the labeling of the effort as a "high-tech gamble." With those millions came expectations, and when test scores did not go up, the community turned sour and voted to not continue the program. This is an unfortunate turn of events. Not only could a BYOD variation of the 1:1 program be continued without additional expense, but it is also clear that the initial expectations for technology were either misplaced or misdirected. Promoting 1:1 based on its potential to improve test scores rather than focusing on what other behaviors and skills the transition to technology hopes to create is a mistake.

It is also interesting to note the language used to describe technology-integration efforts when the standard of measure used is a print-based test. Apparently, having students use computers is "a failure" if they don't raise scores. These statements are made as if it is the technology's fault that the implementation did not have the desired results with a kind of "Well, that didn't work so I think we should go back to books" implication. This is exactly the point of a systems approach; taking a kid's pencil and giving her a laptop without realigning appropriate expectations with the other work processes is the problem. It has nothing to do with the technology.

Although some would like to, we cannot tell the entire world, "Yeah, this computer thing is not working out the way we thought, we should all go back to those stone tablets." There is no going back. As we discussed in Chapter 1, the genie is out of the bottle. The postindustrial world is digital, and that is a fact. Schools will soon be, or soon should be, digital places of learning, preparing kids for active and productive participation in that world. The only choice available is for educational leaders to figure out how to focus and align systems to make the academic digital environment work for our students.

We already know that the print-model school that once served us well is past its prime. It is time to look ahead and leave what was once a good idea behind. If you need any more convincing, consider what Tom Friedman and Michael Mandelbaum say in their new book, *That Used To Be Us*. As a prescription for returning America to prominence, the authors makes the case for the educational shift advocated by Daniel Pink, myself, and others over the last decade. In an interview, Friedman (2011) points out that when you look at the numbers, it has to be clear that America is not going to memorize our way back to the top of the world order. Instead, he declares, "we are going to have to out-think, out-invent and out-create" the competition. The debate can no longer be about whether or not we should replace print with technology. That is wasted time fighting the last war; we need to accept what is evident and move on to what is the most appropriate way to achieve the transition while maintaining high standards and appropriate rigor. We need to assess and hold ourselves accountable for these skills and attributes, as well as the basic content that we know students need along the way.

One of the barriers to pursuing this pathway is that educators are so used to content-focused assessments that they cannot even imagine what a different system might look like. In one of my client districts, we worked together to take the extraordinary step of describing what we thought progress would look like over the years to ensure that we were all accountable for progress. These "learning progress maps" were created using an adaptation of Dr. Gene Hall's innovation configuration mapping process. These documents laid out for everyone what people should expect to see as 1:1 improvement strategies took hold. As an example of what their progress maps looked like, the descriptions for the four indicators of "deepening student ownership of learning" follows. In the sample, descriptions found in the column "Beginning" were meant to illustrate where the district was at the time these maps were written. Successive columns describe stages of progress on the way to "Mastering," which is where they hope to arrive at some point.

Going through a process like this helps to solidify for the entire community the purpose and goals for moving to 1:1. It communicates to others a reason for the digital transition beyond paper-based test

Figure 5.7   Deepening Student Learning Progress Map

I Beginning	II Progressing	III Accomplishing	IV Mastering
1. Without sustained adult intervention, most work processes would not occur.	Most work processes are completed with minor adult intervention or guidance.	Most works processes are completed without adult intervention. Students may seek information, but do so on their own initiative.	Most work processes are completed without adult intervention and are clearly above common expectations for the task at hand. Students seek information and feedback, but do so on their own initiative.
2. Students are not systemically expected to use interpersonal and self-directional (e-learning, time management, calendar, collaboration) tools to enhance productivity and personal development.	Students are infrequently expected to use interpersonal and self-directional (e-learning, time management, calendar, collaboration) tools to enhance productivity and personal development.	Students are occasionally expected to use interpersonal and self-directional (e-learning, time management, calendar, collaboration) tools to enhance productivity and personal development.	Students consistently use interpersonal and self-directional (e-learning, time management, calendar, collaboration) tools to enhance productivity and personal development.
3. Expectations for student technology learning are presented by the teacher. Students are not engaged in setting the criteria.	Teacher generates criteria and rubrics for technology applications to use and posts these in the room. Models of student work are inconsistently used.	Students help to develop the criteria and rubrics for technology applications based on information and examples provided by the teacher. These are clearly posted in room or on the web for references for the duration of the project.	Students help to develop the criteria and rubrics for technology applications based on information and examples provided by the teacher. These are clearly posted in room and on the web or intranet as references for the duration of the project.

4. Models lack authenticity, being teacher generated mock-ups and not actual student products.	Expectations are primarily focused on the end product with few references to intermediate expectations or benchmarks.	There is little emphasis on intermediate expectations or benchmarks. Models of authentic student work are used but sometimes are not completely aligned with the established criteria and rubrics.	Models of authentic student work are displayed and posted on the web that demonstrate progress toward or meet established standards to be used by students to reflect on their own work. Intermediate expectations are also clearly delineated and understood.

scores, which will be critical when you work to align the second set of top-tier systems, instruction, and assessment. The connections between these three systems will be the driving focus of all your leadership work to come. Before we move on, to determine what your school or district's position is in relation to these first two critical systems, on the *Digital Learning for All, Now* webpage, you can find the following self-assessment indicators:

System 1: Leadership and Focus

1.1 Vision and Focus

1.2 Continuous Improvement

1.3 Systems Thinking and Alignment

1.4 Culture and Modeling

System 2: Goals for Learning

2.1 Commitment to Rigor and Understanding

2.2 Articulation of 21st Century Skills

For each downloadable indicator, there are descriptors along a developmental scale and, when appropriate, links to model evidence and strategy prompts for improvement starting points. Also, there is a link to a master profile–creating analysis tool that will take all of your self-assessment results across all eight improvement systems and generate a districtwide "big picture" sense of strengths and weaknesses. A sample of one of these assessment indicators is presented in Figure 5.8.

Figure 5.8 Sample Self-Assessment Indicator

1.4 Culture and Modeling

The culture of your district and schools support and celebrate authentic use of digital tools for learning across the curriculum. These tools are used to advance both administrative and curricular applications. District, building , and instructional leaders have a share vision of a 21st century school system, are conversant regarding opportunity and challenge of one-to-one learning, and are consistently working toward realizing its potential.

0	1	2	3	4

No systematic application	Systemic technology applications
Innovation derided	Innovation celebrated
Haphazard examples	Comprehensive use in all areas
No vision or inconsistent articulation	Vision clear and consistent
Leader's modeling absent	Thoughtful and abundant modeling by leaders
Do As I say, Not as I do	Come join me

Rationale for Score:

Areas of District Strength: *Area Where Growth is Needed:*

If you rated 2 or lower:

- Look in the mirror-how have you modeled or not modeled these expectations?
- Initiate a Professional Learning Community process to explore the rationale for Digital Learning for All, NOW! that is described in Chapter One. Have administrative leaders work through the book's reflection questions.
- Encourage and motivate leaders to demonstrated their ability to live the digital learning vision of the district.

To download an electronic version of this resource so you can adapt it and use it in your own school community, go to **http://www.digitallearningforallnow.com,** click on the "Digital Resources" button, select the appropriate chapter from the drop-down menu, and enter the password **D L F A N** (all uppercase).

Four Foundational Systems:
Part 2—Instruction and Assessment

Whether you select six skill goals for learning or one, the next steps are to align classroom instructional practices and assessment with these outcomes. Of all the alignment issues that should be attended to in a dynamic educational systems orientation, the connection between these two is the most critical. The truism "what gets measured gets done" is the reason why. As we mentioned in the last section, if we profess to want students to master 21st century skills but only report or value print/content-driven test data, then it should not be a surprise that print/content-driven instruction will rule classroom practice. We should not expect any teacher to fall on his sword for having low scores in the name of 21st century learning.

To ensure that students are getting the skill preparation they need, districts must balance their assessment practices to reflect the value balance between content mastery and real-world skills demonstrations. This means reporting on assessment data across the spectrum of learning outcomes. Unfortunately, for as long as they are valued, that does mean you will be accountable for SAT, AP, and other paper-based tests. There is some hope on the horizon as a new generation of digital assessments is on the way that will help balance that. In fact, a consortium of thirty-one states is working on a new Common Core State Standard assessment that will include adaptive digital assessment materials.

The SMARTER Balance adaptive online assessments, planned to launch in 2015, may be the beginning of the end of the paper-based mass assessment (State of Washington Office of the Superintendent of Public Instruction, 2011). Until then, we must report these old results along with locally generated data driven by analytic rubrics associated with 21st century skills. Only with this public sharing of results will teachers have the incentive they need to make the instructional space required for the self-directed inquiry that makes that skill development possible. If the goals for learning are balanced along a content and 21st century skill continuum, so should we see evidence of a similar balance in classroom practice and associated assessment data.

The hard part of achieving this content/skills balance on the instructional and assessment fronts is obviously not on the content side. We have lots of instructional and testing practice in that area. The challenge will be building those open-ended opportunities to help students practice the inquiry-based problem-solving skills that need to be the hallmark of information age learning. In a 1:1 environment, classroom boundaries should be meaningless, and students should be encouraged to take advantage of this extension of the learning environment. It has never been easier or more important to meet students where they are and offer them opportunities to practice and improve on the skills they will need to be successful in the world beyond school. To frame this approach, the following systems-indicator reflections are provided:

System 3: Teaching and Instruction

3.1 Purposeful Alignment

3.2 Higher-Order Engagement

3.2 Rigor, Relevance, and Self-Direction

System 4: Assessment and Data

4.1 Shared and Reliable Assessments

4.2 Deliverables and Evidence

4.3 Timely and Transparent Data

When a district uses these self-assessments to learn of their student's strengths and weaknesses, there are fortunately a multitude of resources available to help staff gain an understanding about what success should look like and how to get there. This is the case because while BYOD is a new phenomenon, 1:1 education is not. For more than a decade, teachers have been experimenting and improving 1:1 instruction and are sharing the techniques that we now must look to scale up for all students.

As a result, there are hundreds of webpages that can guide educators to resources for improving practice in 21st century instruction and assessment. To get you started, on the *Digital Learning for All, Now* webpage, I have posted a downloadable unit/project-planning template (Figure 5.9) that is designed to apply learned content and create 21st century skill experiences. A teacher who designs a project for students with these steps assures that students will practice and apply an array of 21st century skills. By just doing units like these on a regular basis, students will be building competencies that they will need in authentic learning and work settings. The results of these activities carry tangible, observable work products that demonstrate the outcome of instruction. I wonder if the folks who are currently trying to defend their move to 1:1 with only test-score outcomes would benefit from adding student work to their performance reporting.

Figure 5.9   21st Century Project Planning Template

Goals/Objectives (What do you want to learn?)	
Assessment Evidence and Tasks (How will we know you learned it?)	
Authentic Task—RAFT (Role, Audience, Format, Topic)	
Information-Gathering Task (What, where, and how many?)	
Information-Evaluation Activity (What's good and what's not?)	
Information Synthesis (What does it mean and how does it solve or address the problem at hand?)	
Communication of Findings (How will you tell us about what you found?)	
Respond/Reflection (What did you actually learn?)	

Also on the *Digital Learning for All, Now* page are rubrics for measuring skill performance and giving students feedback for many of the 21st century skills we have discussed in this and previous chapters. These rubrics are critical starting points because they provide a mechanism to shift the focus of rigor in your instructional environment. As I indicated in the changing assumptions segment, in a content-focused world, rigor is defined by "how much" you can cram into a brain. In a skill-application setting, the new standard of rigor needs to be "how well" you used what you learned to do something meaningful. Without a standard to judge by, there is no way to help learners understand what good, good enough, or great looks like in these domains. In a precursor to 21st century skills, my friend Bena Kallick and her partner Art Costa (no relation) wrote a helpful series about what they called *habits of mind*. Their ASCD volume on *Assessing & Reporting on Habits of Mind*, which was first published in 2000, has many good ideas about how to approach the assessment of these harder to quantify skills.

Whatever strategies you use, it is critical that you articulate that rigor does not mean only content; skill measurement can be rigorously applied as well. For years, the College Board has been judging good writing through a six-level analytic rubric designed to do exactly this. At EDUCATION CONNECTION, all Center for 21st Century Skill courses involve a culminating challenge project that is judged based on similar skill rubrics. Each spring at our student work expo, we use these rubrics to judge student work and identify excellence. We want our students to know that work quality matters and that assessment in a skill-based-learning world has consequences just as it does in the real world of work. Rigor and high standards are not exclusive domains of traditional testing. Skill-based rubrics like the sample that follows (Figure 5.10) are mechanisms you can use to build a case to help balance the weight of paper-based tests in performance reporting.

At this point, many are probably thinking, "Sure, we would love to do projects and use analytic rubrics to build 21st century skills, but where do we find the time in our curricula for that?" And it is true; we have a hundred-year history of adding stuff to public school curricula and a very limited history of adding time to get any of it done. The solution starts by making hard choices about what content really matters and culminates in the development of highly focused digital curriculum resources. A process that could be used for this was described in the previous chapter.

Figure 5.10   21st Century Assessment Rubric Sample

Item	Insufficient—1	Sufficient—2	Proficient—3	Excellent—4
Identify and ask significant questions that clarify various points of view and lead to better solutions	Either does not formulate questions or the questions generated are irrelevant to the problem.	Questions are relevant to the problem.	Most questions are relevant. The student is able to adjust questions and approaches based on responses and feedback.	Questions are consistently relevant. The student independently adjusts questions based on response and context.
Analyze how parts of a whole interact with each other to produce overall outcomes in complex systems	Analysis not present. Student may understand discrete parts but lacks understanding of how they are connected to whole.	Basic analysis is present. Parts are loosely connected, and there is limited evidence of connecting parts to whole.	Analysis shows an organizational framework by connecting all parts to the whole.	Analysis is insightful, relevant, and comprehensive within an organized framework.
Effectively analyze and evaluate evidence, arguments, claims, and beliefs	Does not evaluate information for relevance or accuracy.	Evaluates information for relevance or accuracy using criteria to make the evaluation.	Accurately evaluates information based on criteria that are clear and reasonable.	Accurately evaluates information based on criteria that are clear, reasonable, and insightful. Distinguishes between claims, beliefs, and empirical evidence.
Synthesize and make connections between information and arguments	No synthesis. Offers summaries of ideas but no explanations or conclusions.	Attempts at synthesis indicated through combining ideas from limited sources. However, no conclusions or generalizations offered.	Conclusions or generalizations offered but not both. Or conclusions and generalizations are drawn directly from sources and do not represent ability to create new ideas.	Synthesis creates new ideas and generalizations based on previous knowledge and experiences. Integrates knowledge from several sources and draws conclusions.

The Next Level: Critical Support Systems—Curriculum and Communication

Even in small districts, classroom teachers do not exist on organizational islands. An instructor may be able to create and implement wonderful hands-on activities that engage and inspire her students without any help or support from those around her. But the bottom line is that eventually, without systemic support, these efforts are doomed to wither and die. There are four support systems on which the top tier rests, and their inclusion in our systems analysis is critical because they are what will sustain your efforts to rethink the student-teacher relationship. Again, using our gears metaphor, the next level systems are curriculum and communication, professional support, professional evaluation, and resource deployment. Our completed graphic of all eight integrated and interrelated systems is seen in Figure 5.11.

The first system we will explore in this second tier is curriculum and communications. As I mentioned at the end of the last section, the curriculum is the place where we make determinations about what we value for learning most and give teachers the direction and resources they need to be successful in leading students to learn it. A well-resourced curriculum framework is the district's or school's best ally in helping teachers avoid falling into old print habits and the dreaded technology retrofit. We know that the textbook is a powerful crutch, and its long-held influence on curriculum and instruction is not open to debate. It is handy and comfortable and as such frequently becomes the default curriculum. When in doubt, follow the text. This dependence and convenience can only be overcome with a curriculum resource that is a better teacher's aide than the textbook itself. To accomplish this, curriculum in a 21st century 1:1 learning environment needs to be digital, easy to access, and resource rich.

Figure 5.11   Eight 21st Century Integrated Systems

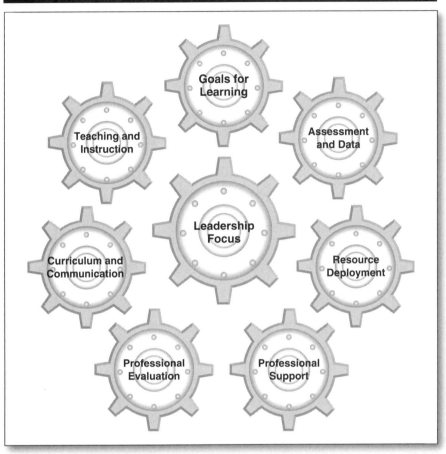

To be attractive, digital curriculum must have integrated lessons and units, links to external resources, aligned assessments, and easy-to-use data collection and analysis tools. Chapter 2 of Heidi Hayes Jacobs's book *Curriculum 21* (2010) does an excellent job of laying out what this upgraded curriculum with integrated assessments should include. To digitally organize and connect all of these materials, districts have a number of choices. It can be done for free in the spirit of the open-source approach we discussed in Chapter 3 and fashioned with just sweat equity.

To accomplish this, a district could construct curricula using Moodle the way we did it for the U.S. history textbook–replacement project I described in Chapter 3 and for several contract courses we have built for customers who wanted stand-alone digital courses. Beyond Moodle, other open-source options for constructing online curricula include

- locally generated interactive webpages—simply create your own webpages/spaces for a course or curriculum area that lay out units and provide hot links to any materials, resources, or assessments that you create within your district or connect to outside;
- joining a general curriculum community or wiki using publicly shared resources through sites like Curriki (http://www.curriki.org/) or Open Planner (http://www.openplanner.org); and
- joining a subject-specific group that focuses open-source sharing on certain subjects like those found at Open Source Physics (http://www.opensourcephysics.org).

I offer one final curriculum-design caution before we move on to the issue of communication. It is true that a curriculum with fewer items to cover but with the resources to teach them more meaningfully for students will result in greater retention and use of those items than an overloaded one requiring more superficial instruction. Less is more if it is done rigorously and in depth. Less content with no rigor and bad instruction is a disaster waiting to happen. This is why effectiveness of the upcoming systems of professional support and professional evaluation are so critical.

In the context of curriculum, communications is equivalent to transparency. One of the great benefits of web-based curriculum is not only its ease of access for teachers but also the way it allows districts to make curriculum accessible to parents and anyone else who is interested. If this seems an odd goal, consider the impact that transparency in curriculum has on its implementation. When everyone knows what the curriculum is and how it is supposed to work, an interesting thing happens: It actually gets taught that way. In transparency, there is accountability for teachers and administrators.

Curriculum documents have always been public documents, but as binders weighing many pounds, the public rarely accessed them. By posting curriculum resources online, parents can easily see what is going on in their student's classes. This encourages dialogue and incentive for the teacher, some might say a little pressure, to do what is called for in the curriculum structure. It may take getting used to, but in the end, it is a good thing for the students and school. Curriculum represents a huge investment of time and resources on the part of the public school community. Anything that encourages these resources to be used in the manner in which they are intended is a positive outcome. By having quality curriculum and communicating its contents through the educational community, teachers create a foundation of trust and partnership with parents that will pay dividends in the long run. Here are the curriculum and communications systems indicators:

System 5: Curriculum and Communications

   5.1 Leading to Learn

   5.2 Resource Rich

   5.3 Transparent and Available

REFLECTION/STUDY QUESTION

How transparent and open are your district's current methods of communication? Are outsiders welcome, and are materials made readily available to parents and members of the public? Your answers will not only have an impact in the realm of making curriculum more accessible, but will also be a predictor of attitudes when it comes to security and equipment availability.

The Next Level: Professional Support, Professional Evaluation, and Resource Deployment

In traditional print contexts, these two areas usually are discussed as professional development and teacher evaluation. I prefer *professional support* and *professional evaluation* because these different terms help to capture the unique challenges of professional educators in this new digital environment. The shift from professional development to professional support is meant to communicate the need for shared responsibility for learning that must be the expectation in a 21st-century school. Too often, when we think of professional development, we think of presentations and workshops that are provided for teachers by the district. This is learning that is done to teachers, not owned or directed by them.

In a digital age, the pace of change is breathtaking, and the use of technology has emerged as form of fluency all its own. Educators, both teachers and administrators, cannot possibly expect to be fluent unless they are investing their own time and energy to learn what needs to be learned. No district has the capacity to provide the professional-development resources needed to achieve fluency separate from individual efforts to move in that direction. Additionally, just as we discussed in the realm of student curriculum, technology learning must be accomplished in a just-in-time context. A district may be able to provide a few workshops on tasks it knows will face everyone, but the majority of technology learning and problem solving will take place in the specific context that cannot possibly be predicted or anticipated.

Skill development and technology learning need to be driven by the self-sufficient adult learner, just as we hope it will be by the student in the classroom. This theme of adults modeling the skills and change we hope to see for our students is the general theme of the final chapter, but the specific point is appropriate here. The district must provide support, and those opportunities must be aligned and focused on the goals of the district; however, the teacher and the administrator must be in charge of their own digital fluency.

In the area of evaluation, it would be unfair to focus this critical system on just teachers when, as we know from our systems approach, adults at every level of the school district play a role in supporting the achievement of students in 21st century skills. Professional evaluation must be purposefully focused on those Pareto principle impacts that we know are most critical for students to succeed in a digital learning environment. Student engagement, rigor, effective balance, and curriculum implementation—all of these factors play a role in student success, and adults at every level should be held accountable for their presence. Evaluative processes must reflect the teacher's craft in fashioning the learning environment as well as the administrator's role in supporting and ensuring that this environment is present for all students.

Unfortunately, in these areas, good models are not as numerous as they are in the areas of curriculum, instruction, assessment, and curriculum. Although it is slowly changing, there is a dearth of effective evaluation models that are designed to specifically support digital classrooms. The International Society for Technology Education's (ISTE) National Educational Technology Standards (NETS) for teachers are probably the best available at this time. Published in 2008, these can be found on ISTE's website (ISTE, 2008). There is a parallel set of standards for administrators on the ISTE site as well.

From my own work, I know that the focus of the ISTE standards on self-direction and student engagement is appropriate; the challenge is integrating this digital mindset into existing process models of professional evaluation. Districts like New Haven, Connecticut, have made news in recent years pioneering evaluation-process models that include student performances and data, but a true digital perspective is lacking. What will make the most sense is the combination of ISTE's technology standards with a solid professional structure applied at both the teacher and administrative levels. To align this critical system with the spirit of a 1:1 learning environment, a concerted effort must be made to rethink the indicators of success that are the foundation of these models to include the Pareto principle behaviors that we know will drive success in a student's acquisition of 21st century skills.

Regardless of the tool or foundational content, as long as the process is focused on 21st century skills and applied through the system, it will have a beneficial support impact on the top-tier systems and the ultimate mission of the district. Here are the individual indicators for these two support systems.

System 6: Professional Support

6.1 Purposeful Alignment

6.2 Multiple Pathways

System 7: Professional Evaluation

7.1 Engagement and Rigor

7.2 Student Performances

The final system in our configuration is all about budgets and money. And it is not about how much money you have; it's about how you align those resources with your goals. Shifting budgeting allocations from print to digital resources is going to be a critical strategy in support of 1:1 in your district. In Chapter 3, I introduced a spending analysis grid that sought to highlight all of the ways you support print-based learning. Driving those resources away from print to their digital counterparts is the focus of this system.

The biggest challenge in accomplishing this task is going to be dealing with the change that this shift in resources is going to cause within your district. All of that money supporting the district's print infrastructure was allocated to different departments and different cost centers. This resource flow has carved out very defined pathways over the decades, and even if little of it is discretionary, it still represents budgets and influence. There will inevitably be people within your system for which these changes are going to be disruptive and problematic. How you deal with or lead these changes will help to make or break the long-term sustainability of your 1:1 effort.

The most effective strategy for avoiding these entanglements is parallel to what we discussed regarding curriculum: transparency of values and focus. Much like the base assumptions that began this chapter, in preparation for shifting the budget focus from print to support of digital learning, ask that submitted budget requests be evaluated through a preset and well-known set of analysis questions. If these types of questions are generated prior to the budgeting process and vetted in the community, everyone knows what the process and priorities are going in. A few sample questions follow:

- How aligned is this purchase with the goal of supporting 21st century skills?
- How does this budget allocation support 1:1 learning?
- If this is a print purchase or allocation, has a digital alternative been sought, and what is the comparison rate per unit?
- If it is an unavoidable print purchase or allocation, what is the plan for avoiding it in the future?

By laying the groundwork and establishing mission-based decision standards, it allows budgetary decisions to be made based on a purpose-driven framework rather than just on historical precedent. I understand that it sounds easy stated this way, but we know that it will not be. The inertia of rest and decades of patterned practice are formidable barriers to success. Chapter 6 is dedicated to building understanding of the change process to assist leaders who are willing to take on the status quo on route to building an effective 1:1 learning environment. First, here are the indicators for System 8.

System 8: Resource Deployment

8.1 Mission Alignment

8.2 Systems Thinking

Figure 5.12 summarizes the eight system shifts that we have explored in Chapter 5.

Figure 5.12   Systems Shift Summary

Go	From	To
The Goal	Credits	True North 21
Instruction	Teacher Centered	Learner Centered
Assessment	Content Heavy	Skills in Context
Curriculum	Static	Adaptive
Resources	Print	Digital
Evaluation	Adult Actions	Engagement
Support	Provided	Self-Directed

REFLECTION/STUDY QUESTION

As you look back on the results of your self-assessments, what do you believe your most important systemic strengths and weaknesses are? What lessons learned can you identify as a result of these reflections? What areas do you believe will most require the support of the change tools from Chapter 6?

CHAPTER SUMMARY: WHAT IS YOUR READINESS FOR REALIGNMENT?

In this chapter, we started with an examination of the three phases of technology integration as an introduction to rethinking the systems that support 1:1 classrooms. Knowing that these systems are based on assumptions that guide their development and processes, we then explored the difference between the assumptions that ground a print-based system and those that should be the foundation of a digital one. With this as a frame of reference, we then explored four primary systems (leadership, goals for learning, instruction, and assessment) and four supporting systems (curriculum and communication, professional support, professional evaluation, and resource deployment) that drive success in the delivery of 1:1 learning. All the way through the chapter, we were introduced to self-assessment indicators that should be used to assess readiness for the shift to a digital learning environment.

Armed with these results, we now move on to the last chapter of *Digital Learning for All, Now*. Chapter 6 will review a series of leadership and support tools that will assist in managing the change from print to digital learning.

6

Leading the Change Process

Modeling the Skills and Behaviors We Expect From Our Students

Staring Into the Abyss

In twenty-five years of working with clients and school leaders, I often observe what I call the *abyss moment* of change. This is the phenomenon that occurs when preparations are complete, it is time to act, to pull the change trigger, and there comes an inevitable moment of leadership hesitation. "Yes, I believe it's the right thing to do, yes, we have done our homework, but still I wonder what will happen, and I worry." It is a natural thing; what we have now is known, what is to come after we move is not. So, not surprisingly, we flinch just as the fun is about to begin. We are standing on the edge of change looking into the abyss of the unknown and we stop for one last moment of contemplation and reconsideration.

I used to be surprised by this hitch in the process. The first time I saw it as a young and naïve consultant, it struck me as astounding. I had been involved in facilitating a six-month process designed to remake the membership of a middle school's teacher teams. The principal was concerned that the rosters had been in place a long time, and a pattern of performance had developed that was not in the best interests of kids. He wanted a fresh start, the staff agreed, and we set out to make the change. We had done all the needed background work, involved staff appropriately to identify team criteria, and built numerous safeguards into the individual selection process. The teams were chosen, announced, and then the grumbling began. It was if all the teachers believed that everyone else's team was the one that needed to be reorganized and that somehow their team would be left untouched. After a week of uproar, the principal reverted to the old team structure and nothing changed.

Similar story lines unfolded in my work with districts doing strategic planning as well. I had planning teams with great data, elegant solutions, and solid strategies. But fast-forward several years post-planning, and evaluations would show that little progress had been made. How could these obvious truths not win out? After having the opportunity to reflect and work with colleagues who had studied the change process, I slowly developed an appreciation for the complexity and challenge of transformations in large organizations. As my friend Dr. Gene Hall from UNLV has famously said, "Change is a process, not an event" (Hall & Hord, 2001, p. 4). Just having a great idea or the right answer is not enough, especially when you are working to shift decades of patterned behavior in schools. In addition to having good reasoning and tactics, leaders of the changes proposed in *Digital Learning for All, Now* need focus, courage, and all of the other 21st century skills that we have so enthusiastically agreed we want our students to have when they leave us.

We started this book with a declaration of the need for 21st century skills for students. We will now finish with an aligned call for similar educator skills within the same system. In the first five chapters, I have put the foundational information needed to move to 1:1 in place. We have reviewed the rationale for change as well as the technical and financial strategies needed to get to there. We examined the barriers to making the transition and the eight systems that need to be aligned to make the change worthwhile. And finally, we did a self-assessment of your school's positional readiness in all of those eight areas. If you have followed along, you are probably preparing for your own abyss moment. To help bolster your courage for the leap, let's look at the role that a personal mastery of 21st century skills can play in providing a comfortable and productive landing.

It is important to remember that there is a reason a consensus has developed on the need for 21st century skills, and there is also a sound rationale for why they look the way they do. Everyone who has studied this topic looks toward a future that is best described as VUCA: volatile, uncertain, complex, and ambiguous (Johansen, 2007). One need only think for a few minutes on the pace of world events over the last few years to confirm the soundness of this prediction. Faced with certain uncertainty, 21st century skill identifiers worked to determine what students would need to learn, adapt, and thrive in that environment. As multiple groups of thoughtful people tackle this task, as always, similar lists emerge. Throughout this book, I have shared the analysis of these efforts that we completed within our organization and the top six skills that came from it. It is from this list that we will draw inspiration for the final piece of the change puzzle needed for *Digital Learning for All, Now.*

21st Century Skills: Modeling the Change We Hope to See

One of Hall and Hord's (2001) basic principles of change is that "an organization does not change until the people within it change." If you are reading this book with the idea that you would like to see your organization change, the first step must be for you to be a model of that change. The skills that will ensure students success in their uncertain futures are the identical set we as adult change agents need to lead schools through the process that will get them ready for it. Adults cannot hope to prepare the next generation of students for a future that requires 21st century skills without modeling and demonstrating these skills themselves. It is ironic it is that so many adults profess their desire to have students learn 21st century skills when everyday they miss opportunities to apply them in their own professional lives. Solve problems, be creative, be flexible, be adaptable; these are all traits required of educators who will be successful in leading the movement from print to a BYOD digital learning environment. We need to model the change we are seeking in our youth.

To demonstrate this, I am going to review each of the 21st century skills from EDUCATION CONNECTION's consensus list that I introduced in Chapter 1. For all of them, I am going to offer three things: (1) a rationale and description of what each skill looks like in a leadership context, (2) possible pathways for improving your own abilities in these areas, and (3) recommended strategies designed to facilitate the change process by exercising that particular skill.

Through this, we will see not only how 21st century skills are what students need to academically master, but also how they can be applied in a real-world setting—your real-world setting. Although the skills are presented in a particular order, that does not imply either level of importance or a sequential schema. All of the skills are interrelated and overlap in practical use. To make this point before I start listing them in order, I would offer Figure 6.1 to demonstrate the integrated nature of 21st century skills.

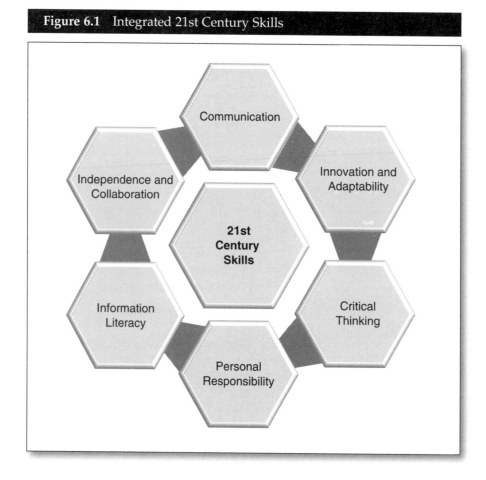

Figure 6.1   Integrated 21st Century Skills

As a way to track your thinking through this exercise, I have provided Figure 6.2 on the *Digital Learning for All, Now* webpage. As you go through the skills, note your own sense of comfort and mastery with each. Which do you believe you already model effectively and which do you think will require the most growth? In the strategies column, keep track of the ideas for supporting the *Digital Learning for All, Now* change process. Adding these strategies to the others proposed in earlier chapters will increase your effectiveness as a leader of change.

Figure 6.2   21st Century Skills Self-Reflection Grid

21st Century Skill	Personal Mastery +/-	Implementation/Modeling Strategies
Communication		
Independence and Collaboration		
Innovation and Adaptability		
Critical Thinking		
Information Literacy		
Personal Responsibility		

To download an electronic version of this resource so you can adapt it and use it in your own school community, go to **http://www.digitallearningforallnow.com,** click on the "Digital Resources" button, select the appropriate chapter from the drop-down menu, and enter the password **D L F A N** (all uppercase).

Skill 1: Communication

Communicate information clearly and effectively using a variety of tools/media in varied contexts for a variety of purposes.

Rationale

Effective communication is a 21st century leadership skill that could have been on a list for leaders of the 14th century. The ability to communicate information to others has always been required for leadership in any context, but it is even more important in support of a successful change process. If you can effectively communicate, you will be more effective in guiding others to understand the rationale, urgency, and outcomes that you all hope to achieve. Variety and context are critical. Leaders must be able to align their message and method for different purposes and audiences. Even if you have an effective message, it will be lost if you make it the same way, every time, every day.

Building Your Skills

Reflect on your current methods of communication. Do you frequently deliver the same message the same way? Is it only about you? Have you fallen in love with PowerPoint? How much variety is there in your communication pathways? Make conscious decisions to stretch into new methods and involve others. Try a Prezi presentation instead, start a blog, use a tool that you have never tried. Ask peers for effectiveness feedback. How good are you at focusing and delivering the message that you want? When messages have high importance, select multiple methods (spoken, written, multimedia, interactive) and audiences to share it.

Supporting the Change

While strategically, everyone needs to be involved in the change process, leaders have a particular communication responsibility. Especially as it relates to communicating the following two areas:

1. *Communicate a purpose and make a case for change.* The bottom line is that we are going to be asking folks to work differently than they have been before, and this process is going to require effort on their part. We know this is going to create a series of personal challenges and concerns, which we will explore further in Skill 6, but for communication purposes, suffice it to say that we need to make clear why we are moving from print to digital. What are the compelling reasons, what is the evidence, and why does this path forward make more sense for students than the one we are on? Joel Barker (1993) said in his groundbreaking work on paradigms that if "you have to convince someone based on the numbers, you will never have enough." Leaders have to be able to communicate the rationale for change on a personal level that speaks to alignment with fundamental principles and beliefs; what can you do to communicate this change as a calling, as a matter of professional responsibility?

21st century communications skills call on learners to understand what the message is and to pick the right tools to deliver the message given the context at hand. Successful change leaders like Ken Freeston in North Salem are known for the consistency and relentlessness of their message whether they are speaking, e-mailing, or simply guiding a conversation. The method can be varied, but the message needs to be consistent. Delivery of purpose cannot be a single speech or one PowerPoint presentation. Impactful mission-driven communication should be consistent, focused, and associated with activities that involve others in experiences that reinforce the message. For this vision of BYOD and 1:1, for example, convene a study group to discuss the points made in this book or others on the topic. Invite people to do research on what students will need to be successful in the 21st century. Success will be determined by the degree to which you can communicate the move to 1:1 as not so much a choice as a clear pathway to the right thing to do.

2. *Communicate a vision and create a common language for change.* From Joel Barker to Jim Collins and countless others, authors and consultants constantly reinforce the importance of vision as a foundational element of organizational success. This is especially true if a foundational change in direction is underway: if you don't have a sense of where you want to go, you cannot possibly get there. Being able to communicate to others what an effective 1:1, post-BYOD learning world looks like is "Step 0" in this process. Without that vision articulated, you may have a small band of pioneers to go with you, but the majority of settlers will hang in the back until they know what the future will look like and that it is safe to proceed (Barker, 1990). This compelling vision and the ability to communicate it to others is a powerful change lever.

The most effective tool that I have seen to operationalize vision is Hall and Hord's (2001) Innovation Configuration Map (ICM). The ICM process allows staff to participate in the creation of a shared vision while at the same time keeping the enterprise grounded in reality. One of the dangers of the "blue sky" visioning process is that groups tend to describe utopic landscapes that are so idealized that they become unconnected to staff experience. The ICM starts by describing what is actually happening right now and then progresses in small steps until the desired state is accurately illustrated. By breaking down the vision descriptions into manageable pieces starting from where you are right now and building toward the goal, ICMs provide a compelling vision of where the process should go without the practical person's disconnect. In addition, they also support the building of a common language through which to discuss the change that is taking place and do so in small segments make effective action planning achievable.

I have used this tool for the last ten years in both strategic planning and BYOD transition planning and have found it equally effective in both. Although Gene Hall and Shirley Hord would certainly not endorse it, if I am very pressed for time with a group, I will limit the number of phases for description to four. I have seen Gene do the process where as many as eight levels of progress are described on the way to the desired state. Regardless of the process you use, this type of structure is an excellent tool for facilitating the communication of vision that is critical to the success of a shift from print to 1:1. An example of a district example of one of my models from the Cromwell Public Schools in Cromwell, Connecticut, follows:

Figure 6.3   Sample Adapted ICM

I Present State	II Beginning	III Progressing	IV Accomplishing
There is no systemic, schoolwide professional development activity or plan for integrating 21st century skills in all disciplines. Community of learning is disjointed and unfocused.	Each content area is having discussions about the implementation of 21st century skills. Certain ideas and models are emerging. Community of learning is starting to focus on similar topics.	Evidence that some teachers are working together to incorporate 21st century skills in their content areas. Learning community is having cross-curricular discussions on similar topics related to 21st century skills.	Evidence that most teachers are working together to consistently and seamlessly incorporate 21st century skills in their content areas. Shared inquiry and coordinated professional learning is evident. Learning community is having a coherent, focused cross-curricular discussion on shared topics of importance to success in 21st century skills.
Current materials and resources are available to support integration of 21st century skills but are not being used consistently.	Teachers are aware of current materials and resources that support integration of 21st century skills and are learning how to use them effectively for instruction.	Teachers are increasingly competent in using current materials and resources to support their instruction, and there is evidence in student work.	Materials and resources to support integration of 21st century skills are available, current, and used by all staff, across the curriculum. Evidence in most student work.

Skill 2: Independence and Collaboration

Work independently and collaboratively to solve problems and accomplish goals.

Rationale

Life, learning, and work in the 21st century depend on patterns of behavior and relationships that are varied and shift from project to project and sometimes even from task to task. The work needs to be purposeful, persistent, and goal oriented, thus demonstrating the importance of aligning work with purpose and forward progress. This requires people to be able to shift from one set of working relationships to another with ease and grace. There will be times when independent work is called for and others when teams or collaborative relationships are what is needed. This will certainly be true in leading this change process.

Building Your Skills

Keep track of the time you spend in both collaborative and independent working environments, and which of them you believe are more associated with goal attainment. Do you know which you enjoy more or less and why? Which is more aligned with goal success and why? Do you have any data to support where you are most skilled or where you might need the most work? Especially for educational leaders, there is a tendency as positional authority increases to become more independent and less likely to be part of productive teams. If this sounds like you, make an effort to stretch into goal processes where you could either use some growth or you know you do not spend a lot of time. Take on tasks or shift strategies to get practice and have reflection time in those areas where you think you could benefit.

Supporting the Change

Be aware of the dynamics of change as you lead and participate in this process. Similar to the first skill of communications, ask yourself, when are the opportunities for you to talk and drive, and what are the times when you should be listening and sharing the load? Demonstrate your ability to step out and take a risk to act independently and then be able to step back and be part of a team solving a problem.

Your role in creating the ICMs described under the first skill of communication can be an example of this. Take it on yourself to get smart on how to create the ICMs and plan for how they can play a role in your specific BYOD change plan. Read, go to training, and develop an understanding of the tool and how it works. Initiate and lead the organization of the ICM work teams, and provide examples and background knowledge. These are all independent actions. Once the process is underway, collaborate and participate with your peers in the creation of those ICMs.

Another excellent opportunity to both lead and participate will be in the reframing of school and district policies that support 1:1. As we discussed in Chapter 4, print-era policies are significant barriers to the implementation of an effective digital learning environment. Use your initiative to get the revision process underway and then participate in the discussion and reframing as a part of the team. Be part of the process, play a role on the team to help them get that job done. Role flexibility on the way to an accomplished goal will be critical to your success in leading the BYOD change.

Skill 3: Innovation and Adaptability

Demonstrate innovation, flexibility, and adaptability in thinking patterns, work habits, and working/learning conditions.

Rationale

In my facilitation work, I often use a data analysis tool that seeks to uncover the most important improvement target that the group does the least well. If this *discrepancy gap analysis* were ever applied to 21st century skills, the attributes of innovation and adaptability would win hands down. With all that we have discussed about the pace of change and future uncertainty, the importance of these skills is hard to doubt. As we move toward an era where conceptual work is going to increase in value, we need to prepare for the revenge of the creative thinker (Pink, 2005). Our challenge is that outside of the art room, most secondary level educators either are at a loss for how to teach or assess for these talents or they harbor skepticism about their importance.

Foundationally, people with these skills are easy to work with because they can adjust to changing conditions. They are unfazed by unexpected events or unusually difficult challenges. When one strategy does not work, they can shift and adapt to another with little frustration. When brainstorming or problem solving, there is evidence of true creative alternatives that come from outside of expected or well-worn patterns of thinking. They voluntarily and happily generate different alternatives and choices. Sometimes frustrating to those who slavishly cling to plans and expectations, innovative and creative learners have a currency with great value in an era of constant change.

Building Your Skills

Benjamin Franklin is credited with the saying, "Three things are extremely hard: diamond, steel, and to know one's self." If creativity and originality are challenging to observe in others, it is even more so to recognize it one's self. Hard, yes, but not impossible. There are hundreds of online self-assessment tools and scholarly articles on the topic. Take a self-assessment, reflect on your own working behaviors, and try to identify your own strengths and weaknesses in these areas. Do unanticipated events give you anxiety? Do you get frustrated when your well-developed plans do not go as you thought? Go talk to an adult or student who strikes you as being a creative person. Talk to her about the way she approaches problems or the creative process. Learn from her. Try something new, try something difficult, and make it a goal to change a well-established pattern. If you are going to convert your school system from print to digital, you are about to ask many of your peers to get out of their comfort zones; you will be a much more effective advocate if you can model that same behavior yourself.

Supporting the Change

When attempting to implement a change on the scale called for in *Digital Learning for All, Now*, I am confident that you will not have to wait long for an opportunity to exercise this skill set. As one of the leading scholars on change Michael Fullan (2001) points out, "a culture of change consists of great rapidity and nonlinearity on one hand and great potential for creative breakthroughs on the other" (p. 31). In other words, if you are going to lead change, you had better be an innovative, adaptable, and flexible person.

My experience suggests that your plan for change will be in place for about ten minutes before something happens that you did not expect. Being thoughtful about how to react positively to this circumstance and model adaptive behaviors will be your best opportunity to ensure the development of these skills in yourself and others. Holding a mirror up to ourselves by being publicly reflective as we go about our business will not only help to reinforce how important this skill set is, but also give everyone an honest assessment of how we are doing modeling this as adults.

In Trilling and Fadel's (2009) book on 21st century skills, they state that an effective way to develop students' skills of flexibility and adaptability is to "challenge student teams to change course when things aren't working well, adapt to new developments in the project, and incorporate new team members on both current and new projects" (pp. 76–77). If I substituted "student" in that sentence with the word "teacher" or "administrator" and then asked everyone to reflect how he or she demonstrated those attributes on the way through the implementation of BYOD, there would plenty of grist for everyone in the flexibility improvement mill.

This process will be especially important for staffs that are wed to certain print practices, or for IT folks, for whom the shift to universal access will be challenging to current expectations. How would encouraging and developing adaptability with these groups help prepare them for these changes? You will have more success if you start small and start in an appropriate context, modeling the change through a practical process that has an actual outcome. Volunteer to try something different, make people aware of what you are thinking, and be a forceful model for change.

As a final thought on this skill, I think there is an important distinction between being flexible and adaptable and being tolerant of low-quality work and careless mistakes. The flexibility associated with caving in because a person is incapable of holding firm to a standard of quality is not what we are looking for here. I believe that highly functional change leaders hold firm to standards of quality and rigor but are flexible about how to get there. It is the same we would expect from teachers in the classroom. Great teachers expect all of their students to succeed but understand that they will take different paths to that success. Commit to the standard and the change but be adaptable when it comes to the pathway to achieving it.

Skill 4: Critical Thinking

Effectively apply the analysis, synthesis, and evaluative
processes that enable productive problem solving.

Rationale

It is a common theme in the new Common Core State Standards: To be successful, students in the 21st century will need to be consistently challenged with "rigorous content and application of knowledge through higher-order skills" (Common Core State Standards

Initiative, 2010). The ability to break a problem down and determine key attributes (analysis), to make judgments and support them (evaluation), and to create new meaning and knowledge (synthesis) on the way to solving problems has always been the hallmark of effective thinkers and leaders. The difference between previous eras and the one we are facing now is the frequency and range of challenges that require these skills. Everyone will need to be able to exercise these skills at some level to be successful. As such, your reasoned and thoughtful modeling of what these talents look like in practice will be a benefit to all.

Building Your Skills

Most school leaders have lots of practice using these skills, but not as much practice teaching them. Accordingly, the best way to enhance skills here is to refine your own understanding of the terms and examples you use in discussing these skills with others. With all of the attention paid to critical thinking skills over the last decade, we end up tossing the term around freely but seldom unpack it in ways that are easy to communicate or share. Much like the clarity of vision issue discussed in the communications skill, without a sharp understanding of what analysis, synthesis, and evaluation look like in the context of problem solving, leaders will be challenged to help teachers translate this into classroom practice.

To improve in this area you could review Costa and Kallick's *Habits of Mind* series, explore the Partnership for 21st Century Skills materials (www.p21.org), review critical-thinking and problem-solving rubrics, and gather good student work examples from your own classrooms. As you construct your mental frameworks, don't lose sight of rigor in this process, as not all problems are created equally. Seek out models of students solving difficult problems and be able to unpack the skills that went into doing so. In the end, you should be able, with great clarity, to speak to the differences between analysis, synthesis, and evaluation, and provide practical examples of they all work together to support effective problem solving.

Supporting the Change

With a tight and focused understanding of this skill in place, you can now effectively model both the content and process of critical problem solving for your staff. We know with a change as complex as the move to 1:1, there will be many opportunities for problem solving. As you proceed and encounter these issues, embrace them, involve others, and enthusiastically make your thinking public. This metacognition strategy, in itself a good model, will help others see how the skills we are trying to teach are applied in real world situations and can lead to better results (Wolf, 2003).

We can anticipate how some of these problem-solving "opportunities" will arise. Inevitably, you will be faced with a colleague who will describe a potential barrier and frame it in terms that imply it is an immovable object that cannot be overcome, thus making this entire process impossible. "Some students will not have Internet access at home." "What happens when the power goes out?" "What will we do when a student's battery runs out during class?" Tackle these problems and work through the process, all the while making the steps and skills used part of the dialogue. Take the lack of Internet access for students at home issue as an example. In one of my early adopting BYOD districts, this issue was raised, and we tackled it together. First, we defined the problem: if we are a digital school and relying on online resources, then lack of Internet access at home becomes a barrier to learning. We then sought out answers to the following questions:

Analysis

1. What is the current percentage of children who do not have access to the Internet at home?

2. How many of those could/would get it if they knew it was important for their child's success in school?

3. What is the actual number gap?

4. What have other communities done to close this gap?

5. What are our options to provide access for those that do not or cannot get it?

6. What are the cost/benefits of the strategies available to us to close that gap?

Synthesis

1. What are the common elements from all of the different solutions we have found?

2. Taking the best elements from the proposed solutions, what two or three options might we construct for own community?

Evaluation

1. Which of these options are the most effective for our community?

2. What do our community peers think about these proposed solutions?

3. How well did the proposals work?

In the end, because the number of students without access was less than a dozen, after exploring the options, the district was able to provide and subsidize 3G wireless networking cards for the impacted students. By making these connections, asking these questions, modeling these behaviors, and leading the problem-solving process for real issues in your community, you give credence and value to the 21st century skill approach. You might even self-evaluate your skills based on the rubrics, like the model introduced in Chapter 5, you use to judge student success in these areas. Regardless of the issue, the more you demonstrate the positive attitude and persistence needed to solve problems and the requisite skills to pull it off, the better your chances of success will be. If you can do it, so can your teachers. And if they can do it, so can their students.

Skill 5: Information Literacy

Use real-world digital and other research tools to access,
evaluate, and effectively apply information appropriate for
authentic tasks.

Rationale

The 21st century skill most directly impacted by the technological changes of the information age, the ability to effectively navigate the torrent of data that flows through the environment, is the white-hot core of our modern lives. As the skill description implies, it is not just one skill but a series of them, and their application overlaps the others on our list as well. Think of how often the attributes involved in information literacy were applied in the previously described problem-solving example. At the heart of this enterprise is defining the purpose of the knowledge task and then going out to find what is needed, sorting through what is found, separating the erroneous from the impactful, and then applying it to fulfill the original purpose. Alignment of an effective information-gathering strategy with purpose is critical, as is the practice of determining reliability and validity of found sources.

Alan November's (2010) warning of a generation of students being raised to be "technology rich, information poor" is worthy of heed here. November has spoken and written prolifically on the dangers of learners who believe that just because they know how to manipulate the hardware and conduct a search, they are therefore masters of the information universe. His portfolio is full of shocking and disheartening examples of students and adults who are supremely confident in what they have found online only to be shown its actual dubious or sinister origin. As November asks in his chapter of Bellanca and Brandt's book *21st Century Skills*, "Why do we teach students to use PowerPoint and wikis before we teach them to be literate in the most powerful information media ever invented?" (p. 276). To avoid becoming an example of this process gone wrong, an effective strategy is to construct a scaffold of criteria that you can use to help students and peers assess the quality of the sources and information they are finding online.

Building Your Skills

There are several resources you can use to help build this evaluation framework, and there are models that you can build on. Many organizations have published checklists and templates for this purpose over the years. If ever there was a 21st century metacognitive learning opportunity, doing a search to find characteristics of reliable searches will be it. Start by completing a background knowledge exercise and brainstorming your own list of attributes of reliable and appropriate source materials. List them in Column 1 of the organizing table that is found in Figure 6.4 and is available for download on the *Digital Learning for All, Now* website. Following your own advice, apply those criteria and research sites that deal with source and search reliability. Find sources to build on what you started. Follow November's (2010) guidance and use multiple search engines and multiple search terms, and always go far beyond the top ten returns on the first screen of results. Did you learn anything that changes your perceptions or original thinking? If so, list those in Column 2 of the organizer. Does what you find agree, disagree, or enhance what you already have? Combine or refine your starting list with the information you found, prioritize the items, and list your new, more robust criteria in Column 3. Use these criteria to guide the research prompts that follow. You can complete a similar exercise with your staff as way to reinforce the importance of this skill.

Figure 6.4 Reliable Sources Research Grid

When researching and evaluating the reliability of online information...

1. My Brainstormed Reliability Criteria	2. Additional Learning	3. Final Prioritized Criteria

Supporting the Change

Similar to the problem-solving process described earlier, supporting the change from print to digital will provide leaders with multiple opportunities to apply and model this information gathering skill. The good news is that through this process, you will find that no matter which issue you are researching, you will find others who faced it as well. These peers have lived through similar challenges and overcome them; all you have to do is find the information about how they did it and learn from them.

You could begin by either sharing the process you went through to determine your own reliability criteria or lead your staff to develop their own. Encouraging staff to do the same with their students or to share the results of similar exercises already completed in their classrooms would add a nice layer of understanding as well. With that complete, you can anticipate research opportunities in each of the following areas of the print-to-digital change process. Results from these searches will allow you and your staff to find the most up-to-date information on solutions and options for successful implementation of your migration efforts.

1. Updated lists of the most successful BYOD implementation sites

2. Literature searches on need for 21st century skill development and 1:1 implementations

3. Lessons learned from successful 1:1 implementations

4. Infrastructure and security options for universal wireless access in a school setting

5. Reviews on hardware and device purchasing

6. Reviews on open-source software options and deployments

7. Identification and evaluation of online curriculum, instruction, and assessment resources

8. Reliable wikis and blogs that share information of pertinent topics

9. "Devil's advocate" sites and articles or collections of inaccurate and misleading information on any of these topics

10. In-context and real-time searches for problem solving information

In pursuing information on these topics, ask that no conclusions or synthesis be offered with fewer than five reliable sources to work from. Ask that resources be prioritized in order of reliability and alignment with purpose and that a rationale be provided. Be sure that your process and questions follow the reliability criteria you established. All of these research and evaluation exercises provide opportunities to once again model for every member of the community what 21st century skills look like when they are applied in a real-world setting. Encourage your staff to take the lessons learned from these tasks as implementers and to use them to increase the rigor of the search techniques they teach their students. Through this recursive modeling and refining, both organizational and student learning will both benefit.

Skill 6: Personal Responsibility

Value and demonstrate personal responsibility, character, cultural understanding, and ethical behavior.

Rationale

With the first five skills listed in this exercise, generally speaking, if there is a deficit, the only damage done is a bad answer or a flawed process that leads to poor work quality. In this domain, mistakes or indiscretions can have profound and long-term damaging consequences. From cheating to bullying and everything in between, allowing students' unfettered access to the information age without a concurrent dialogue about the importance of digital citizenship is tantamount to educational malpractice. Just as we would never give car keys to a teen without teaching and modeling how to drive properly, we should not open the information highway without providing ample opportunity to demonstrate responsible use and making sure our young drivers are wearing their intellectual seatbelts (Adams, 2011). As we discussed in Chapter 4, as we redefine the parameters of use, we need to work with students to help them understand that with freedom comes responsibility. In addition to monitoring and filtering at some level, as educators, we must lead the discussion about personal responsibility and reinforce its importance every day.

Building Your Skills

In the previous five areas, I have promoted the idea of building your own skill and then practicing in public with your staff. In this domain, the process I believe is more internal. I would point you toward a reading from Jim Collins's *Good to Great* (2001) for the reason why. One of Collins's principles for moving organizations from "good to great" is the presence of what he calls "Level 5 leadership." A critical characteristic of leaders at this level of effectiveness is a "compelling modesty." These leaders are capable of looking outside themselves to give others credit, feel empathy, and work with unwavering resolve to accomplish the goals of the organization. To effectively model this most personal of 21st century skills, leaders will need to bring that same sense of openness and connection with others to the interactions they have along the way. Do you see yourself this way? What can you do to increase your level of understanding, respect, responsibility, and empathy for those that you are about to ask on this journey with you?

An effective way to approach this would be to spend some time with Hall and Hord's (2001) Stages of Concern model. Based on years of research and associated with the Concerns-Based Adoption Model, the seven stages of concern map the typical process that people go through when faced with the adoption of a significant change or innovation. Understanding these changes will not only give insight regarding which strategies are most effective in helping your staff move through the process, but it will also give you a sense of why people are reacting the way they are. Honoring those realities is foundational part of respect and empathy for others, which are both components of the personal-responsibility dynamic.

Supporting the Change

No matter how enthusiastically people voice support for this area, remember, if you don't provide a system for people to do the work, the work will not get done. You already have behavioral rules that govern the actions of children and adults in your building; there is no need to duplicate them here. Unlike the cognitive skills in this list, which can be tracked and analytically observed, perceptions of personal responsibility are primarily based on beliefs and behavior. As such, this area demands a different framework for modeling and open reflection. In my work with high schools that have identified responsibility as a behavior worthy of tracking, I have suggested a purely reflective process as the most practical method to encourage the level of thinking needed to improve student actions. This approach encourages a student to internalize the local socially constructed standard and provide evidence of how he believes he has either followed or not followed what the community wanted. An example of this kind of framework is posted in Figure 6.5.

Figure 6.5   Personal Behavior Self-Reflection Framework

Skill/Indicator	Examples	Observations/ Evidence	Comments/ Reflections
Acts responsibly with the interests of the larger community in mind **Is responsible for one's behavior and its effect on the community**	• Follows through on personal commitments or obligations • Accepts responsibility for personal actions and behavior • Demonstrates social and academic responsibility • Does not blame others for personal performance • Accepts responsibility and restitution • Admits mistakes • Is a dependable member of a team or group		
Shows respect for all members of the community	• Never abuses or damages property • Keeps equipment, personal property, and school-related items in good condition • Respects others' wishes regarding personal space and physical contact		
Demonstrates empathy for others	• Does not engage in abusive behavior toward self or others • Cares and supports others in need • Expresses concern for others		
Embraces and respects all identities and cultures	• Does not use insults or prejudicial remarks • Welcomes diversity • Is able to articulate the differences and contributions of cultures and identities not his/her own. • Respects and accepts all members of the community • Is able to interact with others who have different values without conflict		

(Continued)

Figure 6.5   (Continued)

Skill/Indicator	Examples	Observations/ Evidence	Comments/ Reflections
Acts consistently with personal and community values	• Can articulate values • Is willing to express and defend opinions in situations where values play a role • Is aware of community values • Acts consistently with community values • Always represents work of self and others in an honest fashion • Is true to own personality and history • Behaves consistently, regardless of audience		

In this framework, the first column contains the broad indicators of behavior we would expect to see in an in individual who was acting responsibly. In the second column are examples of what this might look like in practice. The student learner then fills in the third column with her own examples of how she did or did not comport herself in a fashion consistent with the indicator or the evidence examples. These reflections can be accompanied by a written rationale. The fourth column would be filled in by an adult to comment on the quality of the observations, not the quality of the behavior. Judgments on behavior are avoided here because those judgments have already been made via the school's already-existing rules and regulations. This is not about whether you have earned a detention or not, but rather, it is about why detention exists in the first place.

To build leadership skills in this area, you can model the value of this process by encouraging your staff to participate in a similar exercise related to faculty professional behavior in this change process. If staff were to fill this out with descriptors for demonstrating professional responsibility in the presence of their peers during faculty meetings, what would that look like, and what would the results be? For students, completing this exercise can be completed as part of student portfolio in an advisory setting or as part of a regularly scheduled project assignment.

In this review of the rationale, skill building, and application for each of our consensus 21st century skills, I demonstrated how these skills are more than just theoretical constructs, but rather foundational components of leadership and learning success. Moving to 1:1 is not only an imperative change that we need to make in all public schools, but the entire process will also be an excellent opportunity to model the skills and rationale for why the transition is needed. All that is left now is to start the process.

Conclusion

If you have agreed with the main ideas of *Digital Learning for All, Now*, my guess is that over the last couple of years, you have had one of Malcolm Gladwell's (2005) blink moments as you sensed the "intuitive repulsion" of asking kids to work in a print world as a way to prepare them for a digital future. Deep down, you know it is not right and that there is something fundamentally out of alignment between the student's world of school and his life beyond it. Frustratingly, for years, the financial and technical barriers to improving that alignment were so great that they overwhelmed our instincts for change. As we have seen, those barriers have fallen. Any district can pursue these affordable and responsible strategies and accomplish this once-in-a-generation change. It won't be easy, and there will be many unknowns that you will need to deal with along the way, but that is all right. The path is open and beckoning, the future awaits; all it takes is action.

Figure 6.6 is a summary of all of the information in *Digital Learning for All, Now*, laid out in a three-phase planning model. You can download an aligned grid from the webpage. The knowledge is there, the purpose is clear; use the tools at your disposal to make the change.

As Fullan (2001) states, effective change leadership requires a sense of moral purpose. I believe that remaking public schools as digital learning environments is our generation's most important moral challenge. It is our defining moment as educational leaders. We cannot allow another generation of students to go through our schools without the tools and skills we know they must master to be successful once they leave. We can do it, we must do it. The future is within our reach; it is time for *Digital Learning for All, Now*.

Figure 6.6   Three-Phase Implementation Plan

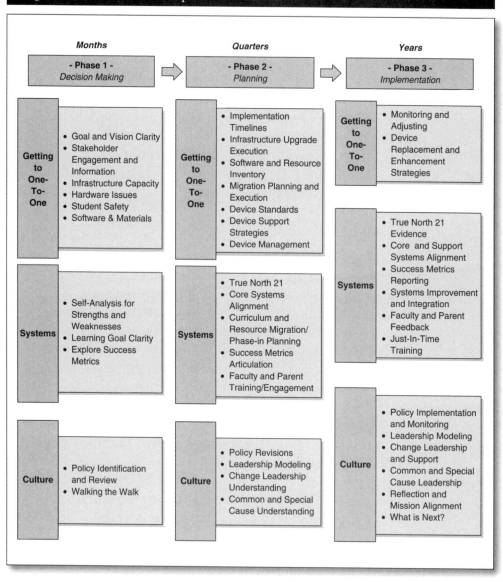

Glossary of Terms

1:1: an instructional arrangement where every student has ownership and access to a digital device whenever it is needed. 1:1 models allow instructional designers to assume that the student has access to their technology 24/7. This shifts the focus of design from the traditional scarcity model where students only have access while in a computer lab or in an area of the school that is equipped for them only during the period they are there.

21st century skills: any defined set of higher-order information-processing, thinking, creation, and communication skills that students require for successful participation in life, learning, and work beyond school.

Acceptable risk: the understanding that in real-world situations, zero risk is an unattainable and unsustainable goal, so we must prepare for an environment that actively manages risk and trains users how to operate safely and securely.

BYOD (Bring Your Own Device): a hardware-acquisition strategy where districts/schools allow students bring their own personal hardware devices to school for official use in school-sanctioned learning and work processes.

Buffer pool: a stable of devices that students can borrow from if their device is either forgotten for the day, lacking a power charge, being repaired, or out of commission for any other reason.

CIPA (Children's Internet Protection Act). Debated and passed in 2001–2003, CIPA provides Internet-filtering guidance to schools and requires them to comply to be eligible for E-rate reimbursement.

Cloud/Cloud based: Off-site server storage or hosting through the Internet. Applications that store data or are run from remote servers and do not require any local hardware assets are said to be run from "the cloud." In actuality, they are based on a server in a remote location removed from your facility.

Common cause: those factors that are predictable and known because they are created by the system itself. Because they are predictable and known, they are therefore also under the control of the system.

Common Core State Standards. Sponsored by the National Governors Association, the Common Core State Standards are designed as a national curriculum benchmark to provide a common lens through which states can compare performance and raise standards for all children. At the time of publication, forty-one states had adopted these new standards, and a consortium of state school personnel was working on an assessment to measure student performance on them.

Crowdsource: any hardware- or knowledge-acquisition strategy that allows/depends on the general population to be the provider of the commodity.

Device agnosticism: a hardware-acquisition strategy that does not require or commit to any one specific kind of technology device, therefore allowing participants to choose the kind of device that works best for them.

Digital learning: the combination of 1:1 access (every student with a device) and electronic materials that enables a shift to completely digital, nonprint learning resources.

Engagement: the degree to which the learner is meaningfully involved in a task or process designed to teach a specific skill or learning outcome.

Equity gap: the skill and practice gulf that exists between students who come from well-resourced families or districts and have consistent access to digital tools for learning and those who do not.

E-rate. Supervised by the Universal Service Administration Company, E-rate funding is designed to support the access of all communities to high-speed Internet service. Schools who comply with the guidelines may receive reimbursements for high-speed Internet service and also for wiring upgrades designed to support it.

Fluency: a level of comfort in use in a skill area that allows application to be done without conscious effort.

Higher-order thinking: the top tier of Bloom's Taxonomy—analysis, synthesis, evaluation, and creativity. Complex, abstract, and rigorous thinking. In the context of critical thinking, these skills are associated with deductive reasoning, driving through the available options to workable solutions. In the context of creativity and adaptability, these skills are associated with seeing new possibilities, creating new ideas of value, and broadening the possible field of opportunity.

Information literacy: the skills required to successfully navigate the information stream. Understanding purpose, creating acquisition strategies, and acquiring, evaluating, synthesizing, and applying the acquired information.

Moore's Law states that the number of transistors on a chip will double about every two years. Intel has kept that pace for over forty years, providing more functions on a chip at significantly lower cost per function.

NAC (Network Access Control) device: a piece of hardware that serves as a gateway to a secure network.

Open source. Originally descriptive of making lines of software code available to the public for development purposes, *open source* has become an umbrella term that covers any software program or resource that is shared freely without license fees.

Pareto principle. The statistical construct named after Wilfred Pareto, this notion demonstrates that in any system of work, a few critical root causes (20 percent) are responsible for most (80 percent) of the outcomes of that system. Also known as *the law of the vital few*.

Proprietary software: any piece of software that requires users to by licenses for its legal use.

Responsible use: the understanding that it is not enough to just teach learners how to use technology but that they must also be taught how to use it responsibly, ethically, and appropriately.

Scarcity model: any instructional arrangement where students only have access to instructional technology provided to them when in certain places in the school. In a scarcity model, students do not own or control their own devices; they must be signed in or out or borrowed for the duration of the period or project.

Single-use hardware: any device that was designed to perform just one function

Special cause: those factors that are random and unknown because they are outside the predictable range of the system's performance. Because they are not predictable and are therefore unknown, they are not under the control of the system.

Systems: any series of work processes that are designed to produce a specific outcome. Typically thought of the way the work is done, systems of work define not only how but also how well work is accomplished. *Systems thinking* refers to the broader strategic thinking that goes into planning how various work systems within a given organization work together to accomplish the mission and goals of that organization.

Vital few. The common application of the Pareto principle, this notion demonstrates that in any system of work, a few critical root causes (20 percent) are responsible for most (80 percent) of the outcomes of that system. The implication is that to be productive problem solvers or improvement facilitators, one must focus on those vital few issues that drive most of your performance indicators.

Web 2.0 tools: a family of browser-based applications that are designed to be used in device-agnostic settings. These tools are designed to be flexible—stressing multiple device utility over installation and device-specific features.

Wiki: a free, open-source-inspired, web-based sharing location where users post and exchange information on specific topics.

References

Adams, B. (2011, July 19). *Be safe and teach them to drive*. Retrieved September 10, 2011, from the Connected Principles website: http://www.connected principals.com/archives/4074

Alexa. (2011, July 1). *Top sites: The top 500 sites on the web*. Retrieved July 29, 2011, from http://www.alexa.com/topsites

Allen, E. I. (2010, November). *Class differences: Online education in the United States*. Retrieved August 31, 2011, from the Sloan Consortium website: http://sloanconsortium.org/publications/survey/class_differences

Barker, J. (1990). *Power of vision*. New York.

Barker, J. (1993). *Paradigms: The business of discovering the future*. New York: HarperBusiness.

Berger, K. (2011, May 19). [Interview with Berj Akian as part of Classlink webinar on BYOB]. Author's personal notes.

Block, C. R., & Paris, S. R. (2008). *Comprehension instruction: Research based strategies*. New York: The Guilford Press.

Bush, J., & Wise, B. (2010, December 1). *Digital learning now!* Retrieved November 10, 2011, from the Foundation for Excellence in Education website: www.excelined.org/Docs/Digital%20Learning%20Now%20 Report%20FINAL.pdf

Coleman, D., & Pimentel, S. (2011, June 21). *Publishers criteria for the common core standards in English language arts and literacy, Grades 3–12*. Retrieved August 16, 2011 from the Common Core Standards website: http:// www.corestandards.org/assets/Publishers_Criteria_for_3-12.pdf

Collins, J. (2001). *Good to great*. New York: HarperCollins.

Common Core State Standards Initiative. (2010). *About the standards*. Retrieved September 9, 2011, from http://www.corestandards.org/ about-the-standards

Costa, A. L., & Kallick, B. (2000). *Assessing & reporting on habits of mind*. Alexandria, VA: Association for Supervision and Curriculum Development.

Cubberly, E. P. (1919). *Public education in the United States*. New York: Houghton Mifflin Company.

Deming, W. E. (1982). *Out of the crisis*. Cambridge: MIT Press.

D'Orio, W. (2008, September/October). One laptop, one child. *Administrator Magazine*, 42–48.

Freeston, K. R., & Hibbard, K. M. (2009, July). *Mission and beliefs*. Retrieved November 19, 2011, from the North Salem General School District website: http://www.northsalemschools.org/district/mission_and_beliefs strategies

Friedman, T. (2011, September 4). Interview by D. Gregory. *MSNBC: Meet The Press*. New York. Transcript available at http://www.msnbc.msn.com/id/44391034/ns/meet_the_press-transcripts/t/meet-press-transcript-september/#.TsUhg3Egd4w

Fullan, M. (2001). *Leading in a culture of change*. San Francisco: Jossey-Bass.

Gladwell, M. (2005). *Blink*. New York: Little, Brown and Company.

Goldratt, E. M., & Cox, J. (1984). *The goal: The process of ongoing improvement.* New York: North River Press

Goodman, G. (2005, October 10). School laptops: Save or delete? *iHerald.* Retrieved August 27, 2011, from http://www.maine.gov/mlti/articles/pressherald/10.10.2005.pdf

Google. (2009). *Corporate information*. Retrieved July 29, 2011, from http://www.google.com/intl/en/about/corporate/company/

Google. (2011). *Customer map.* Retrieved August 14, 2011, from the Google Apps for Education website: http://www.google.com/apps/intl/en/edu/customer_list.html

Gutnick, A. L., Robb, M., Takeuchi, L., & Kotler, J. (2010). *Always connected: The new digital media habits of young children.* New York: The Joan Ganz Cooney Center at Sesame Workshop.

Hall, G. E., & Hord, S. M. (2001). *Implementing change: Patterns, principles and potholes.* Boston: Allyn and Bacon.

Harris Interactive. (2008, August). *Cell phones key to teens' social lives.* Retrieved April 18, 2011, from Marketing Charts website: http://www.marketingcharts.com/ interactive/cell-phones-key-to-teens-social-lives-47-can-text-with-eyes-closed-6126/

Heifetz, R. A., & Lauri, D. L. (1997, January). The work of leadership. *Harvard Business Review Magazine*, December 2001. Retrieved August 21, 2011, from http://hbr.org/2001/12/the-work-of-leadership/ar/1

Hotchkiss, W. A. (2010, December 31). *Slave codes of the State of Georgia, 1848.* University of Dayton: Race, Racism and the Law: Speaking Truth to Power! Retrieved August 22, 2011, from http://academic.udayton.edu/race/02rights/slavelaw.htm (Original work published 1848)

InfoExpress. (2010). Dynamic NAC Suite Network Access Control: Full featured NAC in an hour. Retrieved May 1, 2011, from http://www.infoexpress.com/media/products/dnacdatasheet51_070226-all.pdf

Intel. (2005). *Moore's Law.* Retrieved April 20, 2011, from the Intel Museum website: ftp://download.intel.com/museum/Moores_Law/Printed_Materials/Moores_Law_2pg.pdf

Intel. (2010, June). *Intel corporate.* Retrieved July 28, 2011, from the Intel Architecture and Silicone Technology website: http://www.intel.com/technology/mooreslaw/

International Society for Technology Education (ISTE). (2008). *National education technology standards.* Retrieved November 17, 2011, from http://www.iste.org/standards/nets-for-teachers/nets-for-teachers-2008.aspx

Jacobs, H. H. (2010). *Curriculum 21: Essential education for a changing world.* Alexandria, VA: ASCD.

Johansen, B. (2007). *Get there early: Sensing the future to compete in the present.* San Francisco: Berrett-Koehler.

Jukes, I. (2005, October). *From Gutenberg to Gates to Google (and beyond . . . .): Education for the on-line world.* Retrieved September 18, 2011, from the International Baccalaureate Online website: http://www.ibo.org/ibap/conference/documents/IanJukes-FromGutenbergtoGatestoGoogleand Beyond1.pdf

Kennedy Manzo, K. (2009, October 14). A wider view. *Education Week: Digital Directions Supplement.* Retrieved July 15, 2011, from http://www .edweek.org/dd/articles/2009/10/21/01filter.h03.html

Lenhart, A., Purcell, K., Smith, A., & Zickuhr, K. (2010, February 3). *Social media and young adults.* Retrieved November 16, 2011, from the Pew Internet and the American Life Project website: http://www.pewinternet .org/Reports/2010/Social-Media-and-Young-Adults/Part-2/1-Cell -phones.aspx

Linder, D. (2002). *The trial of Galileo.* Retrieved August 22, 2011, from the University of Missouri–Kansas City School of Law website: http://law2 .umkc.edu/faculty/projects/ftrials/galileo/galileoaccount.html

Livingston, P. (2009). *1-to-1 learning: Laptop programs that work* (2nd ed.). Eugene, OR: International Society for Technology Education.

McPhail, J. (2011, May 2). Bring Your Own Device Webinar.

MIT OpenCourseWare. (n.d.). *About.* Retrieved August 25, 2011, from http://ocw.mit.edu/about/

National Center for Education Statistics. (2002, May). Table 5: Average public school size. In *NCES Statistical Analysis Report.* Retrieved April 16, 2011, from http://nces.ed.gov/pubs2002/overview/table5.asp

New England Association of Schools and Colleges. (2011). *2011 standards for accreditation.* Retrieved August 1, 2011, from the Commission on Public Secondary Schools website: http://cpss.neasc.org/downloads/2011_ Standards/2011_Standards.pdf

Norris, K., & Soloway, E. (2011, May 1). From banning to BYOD. *District Administration.* Retrieved June 20, 2011, from http://www.district administration.com/viewarticle.aspx?articleid=2790

North Central Regional Education Laboratory (NCREL). (2003). *enGauge: 21st century skills.* Naperville, IL: Author.

November, A. (2010). Technology rich, information poor. In J. A. Bellanca & R. S. Brandt (Eds.), *21st century skills: Rethinking how students learn* (pp. 275–283). Bloomington, IN: Solution Tree Press.

OpenOffice.org. (2011, July 29). *OpenOffice.org history and milestones 1999–2005.* Retrieved August 9, 2011, from http://www.openoffice.org/about_us/ milestones.html

Open Source Initiative. (2007). *History of the OSI.* Retrieved August 8, 2011, from http://www.opensource.org/history

Panzarino, M. (2011, June 30). Huge: Twitter now handles 200 million tweets a day, enough to write a 10 million–page book. *The Next Web.* Retrieved August 28, 2011, from http://thenextweb.com/twitter/2011/06/30/ huge-twitter-now-handles-200-million-tweets-a-day-enough-to-write-a- 10-million-page-book/

Pareto principle. (n.d.). In *Wikipedia.* Retrieved August 22, 2011, from http:// en.wikipedia.org/wiki/Pareto_principle

Pew Internet and American Life Project. (2009, April). Teen gadget owner-ship. *Trend Data for Teens.* Retrieved August 5, 2011, from http://www.pewinternet.org/Static-Pages/Trend-Data-for-Teens/Teen-Gadget-Ownership.aspx

Pink, D. (2005). *A whole new mind.* New York: Riverhead Books.

Project Tomorrow. (2011, February). *Speak Up goes to Washington.* Retrieved April 28, 2011, from http://www.tomorrow.org/speakup/speakup_congress.html

Richtel, M. (2011, September 4). In classroom of future, stagnant scores. *The New York Times,* A1. Available at http://www.nytimes.com/2011/09/04/technology/technology-in-schools-faces-questions-on-value.html?pagewanted=all

Russell, M. A., & Plati, T. (2000, June). *Effects of computer versus paper admin-istrations of state-mandated writing assessment.* Boston: Boston College Technology and Assessment Study Collaborative. Retrieved November 11, 2011, from *www.bc.edu/research/intasc/PDF/ComputerVsPaperStateWriting.pdf*

State of Washington Office of the Superintendent of Public Instruction. (2011, August). Frequently asked questions about the Smarter Balance Assessment Consortium (SBAC). Retrieved September 6, 2011, from http://www.k12.wa.us/SMARTER/FAQ.aspx

Trilling, B., & Fadel, C. (2009). *21st century skills: Learning for life in our times.* San Francisco: Jossey-Bass.

Twitter delivers. (2011, July 18). *Brafton News.* Retrieved August 5, 2011, http://www.brafton.com/news/twitter-delivers-350-billion-daily-tweets

U.S. Department of Education. (2008, August). *E-rate program—discounted telecommunications services.* Retrieved May 1, 2011, from Office of Innovation and Improvement, Office of Non-Public Education website: http://www2.ed.gov/about/offices/list/oii/nonpublic/erate.html

U.S. Department of Education. (2010, November). *National Education Technology Plan.* Retrieved February 14, 2011, from http://www.ed.gov/technology/netp-2010

Wiggins, G., & McTighe, J. (2005). *Understanding by design* (expanded ed.). Alexandria, VA: ASCD/Prentice Hall.

Wolf, S. (2003, June). *The big six information skills as a metacognitive scaffold: A case study.* Retrieved September 10, 2011, from American Association of School Librarians website: http://www.ala.org/ala/mgrps/divs/aasl/aaslpubsandjournals/slmrb/slmrcontents/volume62003/bigsixinformation.cfm#meta

Zibreg, C. (2011, March 18). *Mac App Store software 7x pricier than iPhone apps, 3x than on the iPad.* Retrieved April 20, 2011, from http://9to5mac.com/2011/03/18/mac-app-store-software-7x-pricier-than-iphone-apps-3x-than-on-the-ipad/

Index

CORWIN

A SAGE Company

The Corwin logo—a raven striding across an open book—represents the union of courage and learning. Corwin is committed to improving education for all learners by publishing books and other professional development resources for those serving the field of PreK–12 education. By providing practical, hands-on materials, Corwin continues to carry out the promise of its motto: **"Helping Educators Do Their Work Better."**